Big Book of Animal Trivia: 57 Creatures, 1,000+ Questions

MARK PHILLIPS

Methods and Materials: All correct answers have been verified by World Book Encyclopedia or other reference works. Many of the incorrect multiple choice answers were suggested by Google Bard or other AI platforms.

Cover image courtesy of Freepik.com

ISBN: 9798872046653

A. J. Cornell Publications

CONTENTS

CHAPTER 1. ANT

1. What are large groups of ants called?
    a. Hives
    b. Swarms
    c. Colonies

2. What is the primary function of an ant's antennae?
    a. To touch, taste, and hear
    b. To fly
    c. To swim

3. How many legs does an ant have?
    a. Six
    b. Four
    c. Eight

4. **What can some ants do to protect themselves from attackers?**
   a. Camouflage
   b. Sting or bite
   c. Hide underground

5. **Approximately how much can an ant lift compared to its own weight?**
   a. 30 times its weight
   b. 20 times its weight
   c. 10 times its weight

6. **Where do most ants live?**
   a. In nests in the trees
   b. In caves
   c. Underground in nests

7. **What is the main job of male ants in a colony?**
   a. To mate with queens
   b. To build the nest
   c. To gather food

8. **What is the primary role of queens in an ant colony?**
   a. To build the nest
   b. To defend the nest
   c. To lay eggs

9. **Which type of ants consume aphids' honeydew?**
   a. Army ants
   b. Dairying ants
   c. Slave-making ants

10. **What is the purpose of fungus-growing ants collecting plant matter?**
   a. To build nests
   b. To create barriers against predators
   c. To grow fungi for food

11. **How do harvester ants contribute to their colony's food supply?**
   a. By hunting insects
   b. By farming aphids
   c. By collecting and storing seeds

12. **What important role do ants play in nature?**
   a. Providing shelter for other animals
   b. Controlling insect populations and helping soil health
   c. Serving as pollinators for plants

13. **Which other social insects are closely related to ants?**
   a. Spiders
   b. Bees and wasps
   c. Butterflies

14. **Which ants are primarily responsible for building nests and searching for food in a colony?**
   a. Workers
   b. Males
   c. Queens

15. What do slave-making ants do to expand their workforce?
   a. They capture workers from other colonies
   b. They raid and steal the young from other ant colonies
   c. They trade with other ant colonies

16. How do army ants primarily obtain their food?
   a. By sending out large raiding parties to catch small animals
   b. By foraging for seeds
   c. By stealing crops

17. What do slave-making ants do with the young ants they steal from other colonies?
   a. They use them for building colonies
   b. They release them back into the wild
   c. They raise them as slaves

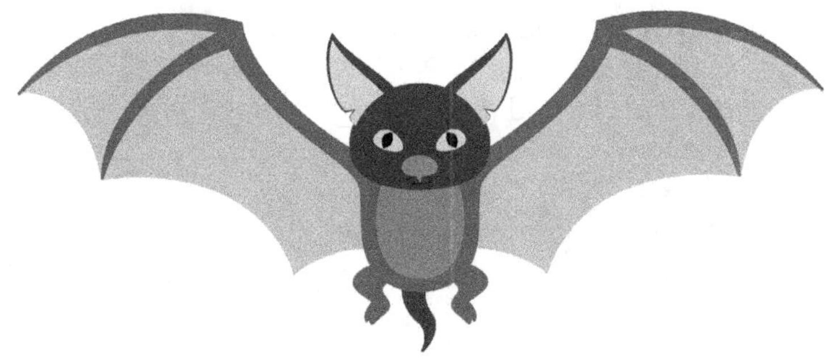

CHAPTER 2. BAT

1. What is unique about bats among mammals?
   a. They can fly
   b. They are the smallest mammals
   c. They hibernate during the winter

2. What do bats feed their young?
   a. Insects
   b. Fish
   c. Milk

3. What are bat wings made of?
   a. Thin skin
   b. Feathers
   c. Scales

4. Where do most bats live?
   a. In the water
   b. In caves and trees
   c. In deserts

5. When do most bats fly?
   a. Only at night
   b. At dawn and dusk
   c. During the day

6. What is the primary diet of most bats?
   a. Fish
   b. Fruit
   c. Insects

7. What do vampire bats typically feed on?
   a. Frogs and mice
   b. Insects
   c. Blood of other animals, often cattle

8. In which regions are most bats found?
   a. Tropics
   b. Antarctica and the Arctic
   c. Deserts

9. What is the largest species of bats called?
   a. Vampire bats
   b. Flying foxes
   c. Bee bats

10. How do bats use echolocation to navigate and locate objects?
   a. They see in the dark
   b. They rely on their sense of smell
   c. They emit high-pitched sounds and listen for echoes

11. What is a common misconception about bats?
a. They have excellent night vision
b. They are blind
c. They are deaf

12. How do bats contribute to the ecosystem?
a. They eat harmful insects
b. They are herbivores
c. They are plant pollinators

13. What has been a significant threat to bat populations in North America?
a. Pesticides
b. White-nose syndrome
c. Habitat loss

14. What is the size of the smallest bat?
a. The size of a bee
b. The size of a crow
c. The size of a rabbit

15. How do flying foxes stand out among bats?
a. They are the fastest flyers
b. They are the smallest bats
c. They have wings that spread about 6 1/2 feet

16. What do bats that eat fruit help spread?
a. Diseases
b. Seeds
c. Pollen

17. **What is the primary function of echolocation for bats?**
   a. It helps them identify other bats
   b. It helps them locate nearby objects
   c. It helps them avoid obstacles

18. **Where are there no bats?**
   a. Antarctica and the Arctic
   b. Rainforests
   c. Deserts

19. **What has led to the decline of many bat populations?**
   a. Climate change
   b. Habitat destruction
   c. Pollution

CHAPTER 3. BEAR

1. What do most bears like to munch on?
    a. Fruit, nuts, leaves, insects, and fish
    b. Meat
    c. Vegetables

2. Which bear species is the largest?
    a. North American grizzly bear
    b. Alaskan brown bear
    c. European brown bear

3. What kind of bear is native to South America?
    a. Polar bear
    b. North American black bear
    c. Spectacled bear

4. **Among North American bears, which one is known for its tree-climbing ability?**
   a. Polar bear
   b. Alaskan brown bear
   c. North American black bear

5. **Which bear species is an excellent swimmer and hunts seals on the Arctic ice?**
   a. Polar bear
   b. Himalayan bear
   c. North American grizzly bear

6. **What is a bear's primary tool for catching prey?**
   a. Sharp claws
   b. Sharp teeth
   c. Speed

7. **How many cubs do mother bears typically give birth to at a time?**
   a. One
   b. Three
   c. Two

8. **What do bears do to prepare for hibernation during the winter?**
   a. Migrate to warmer regions
   b. Sleep and conserve energy
   c. Hunt for extra food

9. **What is the usual den for bears during hibernation?**
   a. Tree
   b. Shallow hole
   c. Cave

10. **In which part of the world do the Himalayan bear, sun bear, and sloth bear live?**
    a. North America
    b. Asia
    c. South America

11. **How long do wild bears typically live?**
    a. More than 30 years
    b. 15 to 20 years
    c. Less than 15 years

12. **Which bear species is known for its distinctive eyeglass-like facial markings?**
    a. Spectacled bear
    b. Polar bear
    c. North American black bear

13. **What kind of food do bears often wade into streams to catch?**
    a. Fish
    b. Plants
    c. Insects

14. **What is the primary hunting technique of polar bears?**
    a. Climbing trees
    b. Catching fish in streams
    c. Hunting seals on the Arctic ice

15. **Which bear is known for being a fierce fighter when angry?**
    a. Polar bear
    b. Alaskan brown bear
    c. European brown bear

16. **What is the term for young bears?**
    a. Kittens
    b. Pups
    c. Cubs

17. **Which bear species is native to Europe and smaller in size?**
    a. European brown bear
    b. Alaskan brown bear
    c. North American black bear

18. **What is the typical disposition of bears?**
    a. Aggressive
    b. Peaceful
    c. Shy

CHAPTER 4. BEE

1. How many legs do bees typically have?
    a. Six
    b. Eight
    c. Four

2. What sweet juice do bees collect from flowers?
    a. Nectar
    b. Pollen
    c. Honey

3. What do bees use nectar for?
    a. Building hives
    b. Making honey
    c. Feeding the queen

4. **What is the process of transferring pollen from one flower to another by bees called?**
   a. Pollination
   b. Germination
   c. Fertilization

5. **Why is pollination important for many plants?**
   a. It helps them find water
   b. It makes flowers smell nice
   c. It enables seed production

6. **How do female bees defend themselves?**
   a. By biting
   b. By making loud sounds
   c. By stinging

7. **What is the term for bees that bite to defend themselves?**
   a. Honey bees
   b. Stingless bees
   c. Solitary bees

8. **How are bees classified into two main groups?**
   a. Worker bees and drone bees
   b. Queen bees and worker bees
   c. Solitary bees and social bees

9. **Where do honeybees typically live?**
   a. In beehives
   b. In underground burrows
   c. In solitary nests

10. **What is the primary role of the queen bee in a hive?**
    a. Collecting nectar
    b. Laying eggs
    c. Guarding the hive

11. **What is the primary job of worker bees in a hive?**
    a. Mating with queens
    b. Gathering food and protecting the hive
    c. Building the hive

12. **What is the primary role of drones in a hive?**
    a. Mating with queens
    b. Building the hive
    c. Collecting pollen

13. **What do people use beeswax for?**
    a. Making honey
    b. Producing electricity
    c. Making candles and other products

14. **Why are bees important to many plants?**
    a. They provide shade to plants
    b. They help with seed production through pollination
    c. They protect plants from pests

15. **What sweet product do people often eat or use in various foods that bees produce?**
    a. Nectar
    b. Pollen
    c. Honey

16. **How do bees help people with crop production?**
    a. They provide natural pest control
    b. They act as scarecrows
    c. They help with irrigation

17. **What is the term for bees that live alone rather than in colonies?**
    a. Honey bees
    b. Worker bees
    c. Solitary bees

CHAPTER 5. BUTTERFLY

1. What is the primary function of a butterfly's antennae?
   a. Smelling, hearing, and feeling
   b. Hearing
   c. Seeing

2. How do most butterflies and moths differ in terms of their antennae?
   a. Only moths have knobbed antennae
   b. Only butterflies have knobbed antennae
   c. Both have knobbed antennae

3. What do butterflies use their long sucking tube for?
   a. To drink nectar from flowers
   b. To eat leaves
   c. To breathe

4. **How many pairs of wings do butterflies have?**
    a. Two
    b. Three
    c. One

5. **What covers a butterfly's wings, giving them their color and patterns?**
    a. Feathers
    b. Fur
    c. Tiny flat scales

6. **What is the first life stage of a butterfly?**
    a. Pupa
    b. Adult
    c. Caterpillar

7. **What do caterpillars use to eat leaves and other plant parts?**
    a. Long sucking tubes
    b. Chewing mouthparts
    c. Proboscises

8. **What is the term for the process in which a caterpillar sheds its old skin and grows new skin?**
    a. Molting
    b. Metamorphosis
    c. Hibernation

9. **What forms around the pupa during its transformation into an adult butterfly?**
   a. A cocoon
   b. A chrysalis
   c. A shell

10. **How do butterflies contribute to the pollination of plants?**
    a. They help plants grow by providing shade
    b. They carry pollen from one flower to another
    c. They spread seeds

11. **How do female butterflies contribute to the next generation?**
    a. By laying eggs
    b. By building nests
    c. By hunting for food

12. **What happens to butterflies soon after they mate?**
    a. They live for many years
    b. They go into hibernation
    c. They usually die

13. **Which caterpillar is considered a crop pest, especially for cabbage and cauliflower?**
    a. Monarch butterfly caterpillar
    b. Swallowtail butterfly caterpillar
    c. Cabbage butterfly caterpillar

14. **What is the purpose of the bright orange color on a monarch butterfly's wings?**
   a. To attract mates
   b. To warn predators that it's poisonous
   c. To camouflage with flowers

15. **How do male monarch butterflies attract females?**
   a. By displaying colorful wings
   b. By singing songs
   c. By releasing scents from black spots on their lower wings

16. **What is the typical wingspan of a monarch butterfly?**
   a. 3 1/2 to 4 inches
   b. 2 inches
   c. 6 inches

17. **Why do monarch butterflies migrate thousands of miles each fall?**
   a. To escape cold winter weather
   b. To mate with other species
   c. To search for new feeding grounds

CHAPTER 6. CAMEL

1. In what type of environment do camels primarily live?
   a. Deserts
   b. Rainforests
   c. Grasslands

2. What are camels commonly used for by people living in deserts?
   a. Carrying heavy loads
   b. Research
   c. Riding

3. How many main kinds of camels are there?
   a. Three
   b. Two
   c. Four

4. What is the name of the camel with one hump?
   a. Arabian camel, or dromedary
   b. Bactrian camel
   c. Llama

5. What is stored in the humps of camels?
   a. Water
   b. Air
   c. Fat

6. How long can a camel go without drinking water?
   a. A few hours
   b. A few weeks
   c. A few days or even months

7. How much water can a thirsty camel drink in a single day?
   a. 5 gallons
   b. 50 gallons
   c. 100 gallons

8. What do camels mainly eat to obtain water in the desert?
   a. Small animals
   b. Insects
   c. Cacti

9. Approximately how tall is a grown camel at the shoulders?
   a. 5 feet
   b. 7 feet
   c. 10 feet

**10. What is the primary purpose of camels' wide
     pads on the bottoms of their feet?**
   a. To walk on loose sand
   b. To help them grip rocks
   c. To make them faster runners

11. How fast can an Arabian camel travel?
   a. 5 miles an hour
   b. 20 miles an hour
   c. 10 miles an hour

**12. What is the woolly, brown covering on the
     body of a camel called?**
   a. Scales
   b. Skin
   c. Fur

13. What is the use of Arabian camels' hair?
   a. Building nests
   b. Making cloth
   c. Weaving baskets

**14. Where can you find feral dromedaries, which
     are domesticated animals that have returned
     to the wild?**
   a. African savannas
   b. Australian deserts
   c. European forests

15. **How many humps does a Bactrian camel have?**
    a. Two
    b. One
    c. Three

16. **What is the primary use of the fat stored in camel humps?**
    a. As insulation from the cold
    b. As a source of energy when food is scarce
    c. As a water reservoir

17. **What is the approximate weight range of a camel?**
    a. 550 to 1,500 pounds
    b. 100 to 300 pounds
    c. 2,000 to 5,000 pounds

18. **What is the primary purpose of camels in Australia?**
    a. To compete in camel racing
    b. To act as pack animals in the outback
    c. To serve as pets

19. **What is the average daily distance an Arabian camel can travel?**
    a. 100 miles
    b. 50 miles
    c. 200 miles

CHAPTER 7. CAT

1. From where did domestic cats descend?
    a. Asia and Africa
    b. Europe and America
    c. Australia and Antarctica

2. How much do most adult cats weigh?
    a. 1 to 5 pounds
    b. 6 to 15 pounds
    c. 16 to 25 pounds

3. What do cats use their claws for?
    a. Defense and catching small animals
    b. Climbing trees
    c. Digging holes

4. **What body part do cats use to get around in the dark?**
    a. Ears
    b. Whiskers
    c. Tongue

5. **What kind of play helps cats learn to be good hunters?**
    a. Running around the house
    b. Playing with toys and suddenly jumping on something
    c. Scratching furniture

6. **What does it mean when a cat rubs against our legs?**
    a. They are trying to trip us
    b. They are trying to scratch us
    c. They are leaving their own scent on us

7. **What does it mean when a cat rolls over on one side and waves its paw?**
    a. It wants to play
    b. It is angry
    c. It is sick

8. **What is a female cat called?**
    a. A duchess
    b. A princess
    c. A queen

9. **What are some of a cat's senses that are better than a human's?**
    a. Taste and smell
    b. Sight and touch
    c. Smell and hearing

10. **Why do cats lick themselves?**
    a. To cool off
    b. To keep clean and get rid of fleas
    c. To mark their territory with a scent

11. **What do cats do to tell other cats what belongs to them?**
    a. They make sounds
    b. They use odors
    c. They move their bodies

12. **How many kittens are in a typical litter?**
    a. 3 to 5
    b. 1 to 2
    c. 6 to 8

13. **How long are kittens born after growing inside the mother?**
    a. About 9 weeks
    b. About 6 weeks
    c. About 12 weeks

14. **When do kittens start to see and hear?**
    a. Within about 6 weeks
    b. Within about 4 weeks
    c. Within about 2 weeks

**15. When can kittens start to be played with by
    their owner?**
    a. When they are about 8 weeks old
    b. When they are about 6 weeks old
    c. When they are about 4 weeks old

16. When does a kitten become an adult cat?
    a. When it is about 1 year old
    b. When it is about 2 years old
    c. When it is about 3 years old

17. How long do most cats live?
    a. 10 to 12 years
    b. 12 to 15 years
    c. 8 to 10 years

CHAPTER 8. CHICKEN

1. What are chickens raised for?
   a. Their meat and eggs
   b. Their feathers
   c. As pets

2. What are male chickens called?
   a. Chicks
   b. Hens
   c. Roosters

3. Can chickens fly?
   a. No, they are completely flightless
   b. Yes, they can fly long distances
   c. Yes, but only short distances

4. **What color is the comb on top of a chicken's head?**
   a. Red
   b. White
   c. Brown

5. **What color is the wattle that hangs from a chicken's neck?**
   a. Red
   b. White
   c. Brown

6. **Where do chickens spend most of their time?**
   a. On the ground
   b. In the air
   c. Sitting on a perch

7. **Chickens were bred from the red jungle fowl of which continent?**
   a. Africa
   b. South America
   c. Asia

8. **What is the average number of eggs a hen produces per year?**
   a. 100
   b. 200
   c. 270

9. **When do hens start laying eggs?**
   a. At about 10 weeks
   b. At about 20 weeks
   c. At about 30 weeks

10. **How long do hens typically produce eggs before being slaughtered?**
    a. 3 years
    b. 2 years
    c. 1 year

11. **How long are chickens raised for their meat before being slaughtered?**
    a. 3 weeks
    b. 7 weeks
    c. 12 weeks

12. **What is the approximate weight range of a chicken?**
    a. 1.1 to 11 pounds
    b. 0.5 to 5.5 pounds
    c. 2.2 to 22 pounds

13. **What are the male and female chickens called, respectively?**
    a. Tom and hen
    b. Cock and pullet
    c. Rooster and hen

14. **What is the main diet of chickens?**
    a. Fruit and vegetables
    b. Insects and seeds
    c. Meat and eggs

15. **How long have people been keeping chickens?**
    a. For hundreds of years
    b. For thousands of years
    c. For millions of years

16. **What is the color of the eggs that most hens lay?**
    a. Gray
    b. White or brown
    c. Yellow

17. **Chickens aren't colorblind; they can see:**
    a. A wider spectrum of colors than humans see, including ultraviolet light
    b. The same colors that humans see
    c. All colors except red and orange

18. **Which of these is *not* true about the social habits of chickens?**
    a. They form complex social hierarchies
    b. They are solitary creatures and prefer isolation
    c. They communicate with their chicks before they hatched

CHAPTER 9. CHIMPANZEE

1. What do chimpanzees use their big toes for?
    a. Grooming each other
    b. Grasping branches
    c. Climbing trees

2. Why do chimpanzees groom each other?
    a. To show affection
    b. To determine who has the most status in the group
    c. To remove dirt, insects, and burs

3. What are chimpanzees ranked among?
    a. The most intelligent of all animals
    b. The most social of all animals
    c. The most dangerous of all animals

4. What do chimpanzees use stones for?
   a. As tools to build nests
   b. As weapons to fight other chimpanzees
   c. As hammers to crack nuts

5. What do chimpanzees use stems for?
   a. To communicate with each other
   b. To groom each other
   c. As a tool, to catch termites

6. How do older chimpanzees teach the young?
   a. By grooming them
   b. By playing games with them
   c. By showing them how to make and use tools

7. How long does a female chimpanzee carry her baby around?
   a. Until the baby is about one year old
   b. Until the baby is about five months old
   c. Until the baby is about two years old

8. Where do chimpanzees mainly live?
   a. In forests
   b. On plains
   c. In mountains

9. About how many African countries do chimpanzees currently inhabit?
   a. 20
   b. 10
   c. 30

10. **Where do the majority of chimpanzees in the United States live?**
   a. Laboratories
   b. Sanctuaries
   c. Zoos

11. **How long can chimpanzees live in the wild?**
   a. Up to 45 years
   b. Up to 30 years
   c. Up to 60 years

12. **What is the main food staple of chimpanzees?**
   a. Fruit
   b. Leaves
   c. Meat

13. **How do chimpanzees build their sleeping nests?**
   a. Using rocks and leaves
   b. Using carefully selected branches and leaves
   c. Using mud and sticks

14. **How do chimpanzees communicate?**
   a. Using gestures, facial expressions, and vocalizations
   b. Using sign language
   c. Using the invisible language of odors

15. **How do chimpanzees show affection for one another?**
   a. By ignoring each other
   b. By embracing, touching hands, and kissing
   c. By fighting

16. What do chimpanzees do when they play?
   a. Cry
   b. Laugh
   c. Scream

17. What is the lifespan of chimpanzees in captivity?
   a. Up to 60 years
   b. Up to 45 years
   c. Up to 30 years

18. What do chimpanzees eat besides fruit?
   a. Meat
   b. Vegetables
   c. Leaves, nuts, seeds, birds' eggs, and insects

19. What is the largest community size of chimpanzees?
   a. A few dozen
   b. A few hundred
   c. A few thousand

CHAPTER 10. CROCODILE

1. How does a crocodile swim?
   a. By moving its legs up and down
   b. By moving its tail from side to side
   c. By undulating its entire body

2. How does the body temperature of a crocodile change?
   a. It changes with the temperature of its surroundings
   b. It changes with the time of day
   c. It remains constant

3. Where are a crocodile's eyes and nostrils located?
   a. On the bottom of its head
   b. On the sides of its head
   c. On the top of its head

4. How does a crocodile catch its prey?
   a. By chasing it down on land
   b. By using its tail to knock it out of the water
   c. By lunging forward and seizing it in its jaws

5. Where do crocodiles lay their eggs?
   a. In water
   b. In nests made of sticks
   c. In sand or in nests made of plants

6. Why do people kill crocodiles?
   a. To use their skins to make shoes and purses
   b. To use their meat for food
   c. To protect other animals from them

7. How many teeth are in a crocodile jaw?
   a. 24
   b. 12
   c. 16

8. Why do crocodiles keep their mouths open while on riverbanks?
   a. To warn enemies
   b. To sleep
   c. To cool off

9. How does a crocodile breathe while underwater?
   a. It has gills.
   b. Its eyes and nostrils are on the top of its head.
   c. It can hold its breath for long periods of time.

10. Do crocodiles provide care for their young?
   a. No.
   b. Yes.
   c. It depends on the species of crocodile.

11. How much pressure can a crocodile's jaws apply per square inch?
   a. 5,000 pounds
   b. 500 pounds
   c. 50,000 pounds

12. Can a crocodile's jaw opening muscles be held shut with just a rubber band or bare hands?
   a. Only with a metal clamp
   b. No
   c. Yes

13. How fast can crocodiles swim in the water?
   a Up to 22 miles per hour
   b. Up to 15 miles per hour
   c. Up to 6 miles per hour

14. Do crocodiles prefer to stay on land or in water?
   a. On land
   b. They spend equal time on land and in water
   c. In water

15. **How long can crocodiles hold their breath underwater?**
    a. 10 minutes
    b. More than an hour
    c. 30 minutes

16. **What do crocodiles swallow to improve digestion?**
    a. Small rocks
    b. Leaves
    c. Fish bones

17. **Are crocodiles mainly nocturnal hunters?**
    a. No
    b. Yes
    c. They hunt equally during the day and night

18. **What is a "death roll" that crocodiles perform?**
    a. A way to overcome prey by clamping down with their jaws and spinning around powerfully
    b. A way to scare off predators
    c. A dance to attract mates

19. **How long can larger crocodiles go without eating a meal?**
    a. A week
    b. Over a year
    c. A month

CHAPTER 11. DEER

1. Do female deer have antlers?
    a. Yes
    b. No
    c. Only in some kinds of deer

2. What are antlers?
    a. Strong, hard layers of skin with a bony core
    b. Part of a deer's skull
    c. A type of horn

3. What are most male deer called?
    a. Bucks
    b. Does
    c. Hinds

4. What are young deer called?
   a. Fawns
   b. Calves
   c. Cubs

5. Where are deer found?
   a. Asia, Europe, and Africa
   b. Asia, Europe, North America, and South
      America
   c. North America and Europe

**6. Which of the following is not a natural habitat
for deer?**
   a. Deserts
   b. Grasslands
   c. Forests

**7. What is the main reason deer have become
pests in some areas?**
   a. They cause car accidents
   b. They carry ticks that spread disease
   c. They destroy crops and other plants

**8. What helps to keep deer numbers under
control in many areas?**
   a. Building fences around crops
   b. Killing the animals that normally eat deer
   c. Hunting by people

9. **What are some kinds of deer that have become
   endangered?**
   a. Colombian white-tailed deer and key deer
   b. Elk and moose
   c. Reindeer and caribou

10. **What threatens endangered deer?**
    a. Illegal hunting and destruction of forests
    b. Overpopulation
    c. Climate change

11. **How many different kinds of deer are there?**
    a. More than 10
    b. Less than 20
    c. More than 30

12. **Where have deer been brought to where they
    did not live naturally?**
    a. Australia, Hawaii, New Guinea, and New
       Zealand
    b. Africa, South America, and Antarctica
    c. Europe, Asia, and North America

13. **Do deer carry ticks?**
    a. No
    b. Yes
    c. Only in some areas

14. **What animals have people killed that normally
    eat deer?**
    a. Coyotes
    b. Bears
    c. Wolves

15. **Why have deer numbers grown too large in some areas?**
    a. Because of climate change
    b. Because people have killed the animals that normally eat deer
    c. Because of overpopulation

16. **Do people continue to hunt deer?**
    a. No
    b. Yes, only for sport
    c. Yes, for sport and for food

17. **What do you call female deer?**
    a. Hinds
    b. Does
    c. Fawns

CHAPTER 12. DOG

1. How long ago were dogs first tamed by humans?
    a. More than 1,000 years ago
    b. More than 5,000 years ago
    c. More than 10,000 years ago

2. What were prehistoric people's original use for dogs?
    a. As pets
    b. As watchdogs and work animals
    c. As hunting companions

3. From what animal do all dogs descend?
    a. Coyotes
    b. Foxes
    c. Wolves

4. What are mixed-breed dogs sometimes called?
   a. Mutts or mongrels
   b. Purebreds
   c. Hybrids

5. What is the smallest dog breed?
   a. Pug
   b. St. Bernard
   c. Chihuahua

6. What are the tallest dog breeds?
   a. Chihuahua and Pug
   b. Irish wolfhound and Great Dane
   c. St. Bernard and Poodle

7. What is the heaviest dog breed?
   a. Chihuahua
   b. Pug
   c. St. Bernard

8. How many kinds of purebred dogs are there?
   a. More than 400
   b. More than 200
   c. More than 100

9. When do puppies open their eyes?
   a. At birth
   b. Two to three weeks after birth
   c. 10 to 15 days after birth

10. When do puppies begin to walk?
   a. 2 to 3 weeks after birth
   b. One month after birth
   c. One week after birth

**11. When do puppies no longer need their
     mother's milk?**
   a. 6 weeks old
   b. 3 weeks old
   c. 12 weeks old

12. When is the best time to adopt a puppy?
   a. Three months old
   b. Six to eight weeks old
   c. Three weeks old

**13. How does a puppy learn to be clean and
     obedient?**
   a. By being punished for doing the wrong thing
   b. By being ignored and left alone
   c. By being praised for doing the right thing at the
      right time and in the right place

14. What is the purpose of brushing a dog's fur?
   a. To make it look pretty
   b. To get fleas and ticks out of the fur
   c. To keep the dog warm

**15. Which dogs usually live longer, small or big
     dogs?**
   a. Small dogs
   b. Big dogs
   c. They live the same amount of time

16. How do dogs cool down when they are hot?
   a. They pant
   b. They sweat
   c. They drink water

17. Why do dogs dig holes?
   a. To bury things
   b. To hide leftover food
   c. To make a bed

18. How well can dogs smell and hear compared to humans?
   a. They smell and hear worse than humans
   b. They smell and hear better than humans
   c. They smell and hear the same as humans

CHAPTER 13. DOLPHIN

1. What type of animal is a dolphin?
    a. A fish
    b. A mammal
    c. An amphibian

2. What is the size range of dolphins?
    a. 1 to 10 feet long
    b. 40 to 60 feet long
    c. 4 to 30 feet long

3. What is the difference between a dolphin and a porpoise?
    a. Dolphins have a beaklike snout, while porpoises have a more rounded snout
    b. Dolphins are smaller than porpoises
    c. Dolphins live in rivers, while porpoises live in oceans

4. What do dolphins eat?
   a. Fish
   b. Plants
   c. Insects

5. What is the function of blubber in dolphins?
   a. To help them swim faster
   b. To help them breathe underwater
   c. To keep them warm

6. What is echolocation?
   a. A way for dolphins to communicate with each
      other
   b. A way for dolphins to see in the dark
   c. A way for dolphins to locate underwater objects
   using sound

7. What is the most common type of dolphin that performs at zoos and aquariums?
   a. Common dolphin
   b. Bottle-nosed dolphin
   c. Killer whale

8. Which type of dolphins is especially endangered?
   a. River dolphin
   b. Bottle-nosed dolphin
   c. Killer whale

9. How long do dolphins stay with their mothers?
   a. 1 year
   b. 2 years
   c. 3 or more years

10. How many stomachs do dolphins have?
    a. One
    b. Two
    c. Three

11. How deep can dolphins dive?
    a. 500 feet
    b. 1,500 feet
    c. 1,000 feet

12. What is the average lifespan of a dolphin?
    a. 17 years
    b. 10 years
    c. 25 years

13. How many species of dolphins are there?
    a. 20
    b. 40
    c. 60

14. What is the name of a group of dolphins?
    a. School
    b. Herd
    c. Pod

15. How do dolphins sleep?
    a. With both halves of their brain
    b. They don't sleep
    c. With one half of their brain

16. What is the largest kind of dolphin?
   a. Killer whale
   b. Bottle-nose dolphin
   c. Common dolphin

17. How fast can some dolphins swim?
   a. 20 miles per hour
   b. 10 miles per hour
   c. 30 miles per hour

18. What is the most common dolphin species?
   a. Common dolphin
   b. Bottle-nose dolphin
   c. Spinner dolphin

CHAPTER 14. DONKEY

1. What is a donkey?
    a. A zebra without stripes
    b. A wild horse
    c. A domesticated ass

2. What is the ancestor of the donkey?
    a. The Arabian horse
    b. The wild ass of northern and northeastern Africa
    c. The pony

3. Where is the domesticated donkey most common?
    a. Southern Asia, southern Europe, and northern Africa
    b. North America, South America, and Central America
    c. Australia, New Zealand, and Antarctica

4. What are burros?

a. A type of donkey that carries materials on its back
b. A type of donkey used for riding
c. A type of donkey that draws carts

5. What happens to a donkey if it is badly treated?

a. It becomes more obedient
b. It becomes stubborn and dull
c. It becomes more energetic

6. What do female donkeys produce?

a. Good meat
b. Good milk
c. Good wool

7. What is a female donkey called?

a. A jenny or a jennet
b. A mare
c. A filly

8. What is the offspring of a male donkey and a female horse called?

a. A pony
b. A hinny
c. A mule

9. What is the hybrid between a male horse and a female donkey called?

a. A hinny
b. A mule
c. A pony

10. What is a donkey doing when it makes a loud, harsh "Ee-Aww" cry?
a. Whinnying
b. Neighing
c. Braying

11. What is the height range of a donkey at the base of the neck?
a. 31 to 63 inches
b 20 to 30 inches
c. 70 to 90 inches

12. What is the life expectancy of working donkeys in the poorest countries?
a. 5 to 8 years
b. 12 to 15 years
c. 20 to 25 years

13. What is the consequence of overfeeding a donkey?
a. It will become lazy
b. It will develop a roll of fat on its neck or hip
c. It will become too tall

14. What do donkeys usually enjoy eating?
a. Meat
b. Grass and hay
c. Fish

**15. In proportion to their size, how do donkeys'
ears compare to those of a horse?**
   a. They are about the same
   b. They are shorter
   c. They are longer

16. Are donkeys social animals?
   a. No, they prefer to be alone
   b. It depends on the breed
   c. Yes, they like company and develop strong
      emotional attachments with other animals

**17. Should donkeys be fitted with iron
   horseshoes?**
   a. Only if they do lots of work on hard surfaces
   b. No
   c. Yes

CHAPTER 15. DUCK

1. What is the outer layer of a duck's feathers called?
   a. Down
   b. Plumage
   c. Quills

2. What do ducks use their webbed feet for?
   a. Walking on land
   b. Swimming and diving
   c. Catching prey

3. What is the name for the type of travel that ducks do when they fly long distances to spend the winter in a warm climate and return in spring?
   a. Migration
   b. Relocation
   c. Immigration

4. What is the main food source for ducks?
   a. Plants and small animals that live in the water
   b. Fish
   c. Insects

5. What is the name for the layer of soft, fluffy feathers under a duck's outer layer of waterproof feathers?
   a. Quills
   b. Plumage
   c. Down

6. How many different kinds of ducks are there?
   a. Hundreds
   b. Dozens
   c. Thousands

7. Where do ducks typically live?
   a. Forests
   b. Ponds and wetlands
   c. Grasslands

8. What kind of bird is a duck?
   a. Waterfowl
   b. Songbird
   c. Gamebird

9. What laws protect ducks and their habitats?
   a. Clean Water Act
   b. Endangered Species Act
   c. Migratory Bird Treaty Act

10. **Where can ducks be found?**
    a. Only in saltwater
    b. In both saltwater and fresh water
    c. Only in fresh water

11. **What is the main difference between ducks and swans and geese?**
    a. Ducks have shorter necks and are smaller.
    b. Ducks have different types of beaks
    c. Ducks have different colors of feathers

12. **What is a baby duck called?**
    a. A duckling
    b. A cygnet
    c. A gosling

13. **What type of duck feeds on the surface of water or on land?**
    a. A diving duck
    b. A dabbling duck
    c. A flightless duck

14. **What is the name of the comb-like structure on the side of a duck's beak?**
    a. Down
    b. Webbing
    c. Pecten

15. **What is the main food source for diving ducks?**
    a. Aquatic plants
    b. Insects and other small invertebrates
    c. Fish and other small animals

16. **What does the word "cosmopolitan" mean in the context of duck distribution?**
   a. Ducks have adapted to living in close proximity to humans
   b. Ducks live in a variety of different habitats, including forests, grasslands, and deserts
   c. Ducks can be found all over the world, except for Antarctica

17. **Which is *not* a reason that stale bread is bad for ducks?**
   a. It can pollute the water
   b. It can cause blockages in their digestive system
   c. It is not nutritious and can lead to malnutrition

CHAPTER 16. ELEPHANT

1. What are the two main kinds of elephants?
   a. African elephants and Asian elephants
   b. African elephants and European elephants
   c. North American elephants and African
      elephants

2. How do Asian elephants differ from African elephants?
   a. They are smaller
   b. They have larger ears
   c. They have larger tusks

3. How much can some elephants weigh?
   a. About 1,000 pounds
   b. About 12,000 pounds
   c. About 5,000 pounds

4. **What is the height of an elephant at the shoulder?**
   a. About 5 feet
   b. About 8 feet
   c. About 11 feet

5. **What do elephants use their trunks for?**
   a. To carry water
   b. To reach tall branches
   c. To carry and eat plant foods

6. **How many pounds of plants do wild elephants eat in a day?**
   a. About 100
   b. About 300
   c. About 200

7. **Do elephants live alone or in groups?**
   a. Alone
   b. In groups
   c. Both, depending on the species

8. **How does an elephant take a shower?**
   a. It suctions water into its trunk and sprays it over its body
   b. It stands under a waterfall
   c. It rolls around in a mud puddle

9. **What is the purpose of an elephant covering itself with dirt after a mud bath?**
   a. For camouflage
   b. To keep warm
   c. To protect its skin from the sun and insects

10. Why do elephants bathe in lakes and rivers?
  a. To cool off
  b. To clean themselves
  c. To drink water

11. How far away can elephants hear each other?
  a. About 2.5 miles
  b. About 5 miles
  c. About 1 mile

12. What are elephant tusks made of?
  a. Bone
  b. Ivory
  c. Tooth enamel

13. Why have people killed many elephants?
  a. To take their meat
  b. To protect their crops
  c. To take their tusks

14. Is hunting elephants legal?
  a. Yes, but only in certain countries
  b. No
  c. Yes, but only with a special permit

15. What is the average lifespan of an African elephant?
  a. 40 to 50 years
  b. 80 to 90 years
  c. 60 to 70 years

16. **What is the average birth weight of an elephant calf?**
    a. 200 to 250 pounds
    b. 150 to 200 pounds
    c. 100 to 150 pounds

17. **How do elephants rank in terms of intelligence among animals?**
    a. They are among the most intelligent animals
    b. They are of average intelligence
    c. They are among the least intelligent animals

CHAPTER 17. FOX

1. Where do foxes *not* live?
   a. North America
   b. Southeast Asia
   c. Antarctica

2. What is the average length of a fox, not counting the tail?
   a. 10 to 15 inches
   b. 30 to 35 inches
   c. 23 to 27 inches

3. How many young do foxes typically have at a time?
   a. 3 to 9
   b. 1 to 2
   c. 10 to 12

4. Do foxes form packs like wolves?
   a. Yes
   b. No
   c. Only during mating season

5. When do female foxes give birth to their young?
   a. In the summer
   b. In late winter or early spring
   c. In the fall

6. What is a baby fox called?
   a. Calf
   b. Lamb
   c. Pup, kit or cub

7. What do foxes eat that can be helpful to farmers?
   a. Mice and rats
   b. Insects
   c. Crops

8. What is the average weight of a fox?
   a. 2 to 5 pounds
   b. 15 to 20 pounds
   c. 8 to 11 pounds

9. What is the purpose of a fox's scent stations?
   a. To communicate with other animals
   b. To attract prey
   c. To mark their territory

10. What is a female fox called?
  a. A vixen
  b. A doe
  c. A she-fox

11. What do foxes eat?
  a. Only fruit and vegetables
  b. Mostly rabbits, squirrels, and mice
  c. Only the remains of dead animals

12. What senses do foxes rely on most for hunting?
  a. Sight and hearing
  b. Hearing and smell
  c. Smell and sight

13. Why do foxes have a distinctive odor?
  a. Because of a scent gland on their tail
  b. Because of their diet
  c. Because of their fur

14. How do foxes communicate with each other?
  a. With body language and facial expressions
  b. With growls, yelps and short yapping barks
  c. With scent stations

15. What do foxes do with their young after they are born?
  a. They raise them in a den
  b. They leave them to fend for themselves
  c. They take them hunting

16. **Why do foxes sometimes stand on their hind
    legs?**
    a. To stretch their legs
    b. To get a better view in tall grass
    c. To mark their territory

17. **How do foxes hunt for ground squirrels or
    woodchucks?**
    a. They lie in wait and pounce on their victim
    b. They chase their victim down
    c. They teamwork with other foxes to hunt their
       victim

CHAPTER 18. FROG

1. Which of the following is *not* a characteristic of frogs?
   a. They have tails
   b. They have thin, moist skin
   c. They have bulging eyes

2. What are the long, strong back legs of frogs used for?
   a. Swimming
   b. Climbing
   c. Jumping

3. Frogs are amphibians, which means that they:
   a. Spend part of their lives in water and part on land
   b. Are cold-blooded
   c. Lay eggs

4. Frog eggs must be laid in water because they would:
   a. Dry out on land
   b. Be eaten by birds
   c. Be too heavy to carry

5. What is the name of the young frog that hatches from an egg?
   a. Froglet
   b. Tadpole
   c. Chick

6. What is the process that a tadpole goes through to transform into an adult frog called?
   a. Growth
   b. Amphibian transformation
   c. Metamorphosis

7. On which continent are frogs not found?
   a. Antarctica
   b. Africa
   c. Australia

8. Where do most adult frogs live?
   a. In hot, dry areas near mountains
   b. In cold, dry areas near deserts
   c. In warm, wet areas near ponds or wetlands

9. What do most frogs eat?
   a. Plants
   b. Insects and other small animals
   c. Other frogs

10. What animals eat frogs?
   a. Cats and dogs
   b. Birds, fish, lizards and snakes
   c. Only other frogs

11. What is a frog's most notable feature?
   a. Tail
   b. Fur
   c. Bulging eyes

12. What does an adult frog use to breathe on land?
   a. Gills
   b. Lungs
   c. Skin

13. What is the largest frog in the world?
   a. Goliath frog
   b. American bullfrog
   c. African clawed frog

14. Approximately how many known species of frogs are there worldwide?
   a. 2,000
   b. 6,000
   c. 4,000

15. How many times their body length can many frogs leap?
   a. 10 times
   b. 30 times
   c. 20 times

16. Frogs are cold-blooded, which means that:
   a. Their body temperature is maintained at a
      constant level
   b. Their body temperature changes with the
      temperature of its surroundings
   c. They are reptiles

**17. Frogs are freshwater creatures; but which of
    the following frogs can live in brackish or
    nearly completely salt waters?**
   a. American bullfrog
   b. Goliath frog
   c. Florida leopard frog

18. What are some threats to frogs?
   a. Destruction of forests, disease and water
      pollution
   b. Overpopulation, drought and cold weather
   c. Lack of food, too much sunlight and noise
      pollution

CHAPTER 19. GIRAFFE

1. Giraffes are found in which continent?
   a. South America
   b. Asia
   c. Africa

2. How many bones are in a giraffe's neck?
   a. Seven
   b. Ten
   c. Fifteen

3. What is the name of a baby giraffe?
   a. Cub
   b. Calf
   c. Foal

4. **What is the approximate weight of a newborn giraffe?**
    a. 50 pounds
    b. 220 pounds
    c. 150 pounds

5. **What is the approximate height of a newborn giraffe?**
    a. Six feet
    b. Four feet
    c. Two feet

6. **How long does a giraffe calf stay with its mother?**
    a. One and a half years
    b. One year
    c. Six months

7. **When does a giraffe become mature?**
    a. Two years
    b. Six years
    c. Four years

8. **Why do female giraffes prefer males with longer and stronger necks?**
    a. Because they are more physically attractive
    b. Because they are more likely to pass on their genes
    c. Because they are better at fighting predators

9. **About how many subspecies of giraffes are there?**
   a. Nine
   b. Five
   c. Twelve

10. **What is the average lifespan of a giraffe in the wild?**
    a. 30 years
    b. 25 years
    c. 35 years

11. **What is the average lifespan of a giraffe in captivity?**
    a. 30 years
    b. 40 years
    c. 35 years

12. **What is the main food source of giraffes?**
    a. Fruit
    b. Leaves
    c. Grass

13. **How do giraffes keep predators away?**
    a. By kicking with their feet
    b. By butting with their head and neck
    c. By biting with their teeth

14. **What is a mixed breed giraffe called?**
    a. Crossbreed
    b. Hybrid
    c. Mutt

15. How long can a giraffe go without water?
  a. Many days
  b. Many months
  c. Many weeks

16. What is the purpose of a giraffe's patchlike markings?
  a. To protect them by making them hard to see when they stand among trees
  b. To attract mates
  c. To regulate body temperature

17. How do giraffes walk?
  a. By moving the front legs together and then the back legs together
  b. By moving both legs on one side of the body together and then moving the legs on the other side together
  c. By moving each leg independently

18. About how long can a giraffe's tongue grow?
  a. 12 inches
  b. 24 inches
  c. 18 inches

CHAPTER 20. GOAT

1. How long have people been raising goats?
    a. For more than 9,000 years
    b. For more than 5,000 years
    c. For more than 2,000 years

2. Where were goats probably first domesticated?
    a. Africa and the Middle East
    b. Asia and the Mediterranean region
    c. Europe and North America

3. What is a goat's body covered with?
    a. Hair
    b. Fur
    c. Wool

4. **How many toes does a goat have on each hoof?**
    a. Two
    b. Four
    c. Six

5. **What is a baby goat called?**
    a. Calf
    b. Kid
    c. Foal

6. **Where do wild goats typically live?**
    a. Hot and dry areas, favoring mountain regions
    b. Cold and wet areas, favoring forests and
       swamps
    c. Temperate climates, favoring grasslands and
       meadows

7. **What unique physical feature do goats have?**
    a. Cloven hooves
    b. Rectangular irises
    c. Long tails

8. **What is the usual position of a goat's tail?**
    a. Straight up
    b. Curled up
    c. Straight down

9. **Do most goats have horns?**
    a. No
    b. Yes
    c. Only males have horns

10. **How many breeds of domestic goats are there?**
    a. Thousands
    b. Dozens
    c. Hundreds

11. **How long is the average adult goat?**
    a. 12 to 24 inches
    b. 28 to 48 inches
    c. 48 to 72 inches

12. **What does an adult goat typically weigh?**
    a. 50 to 70 pounds
    b. 150 to 200 pounds
    c. 100 to 120 pounds

13. **What is a goat's diet typically include?**
    a. Grass, leaves and shrubs
    b. Meat, fish and eggs
    c. Grains, fruits and vegetables

14. **What do some ranchers use goats to do?**
    a. Help to spread seeds
    b. Guard their livestock from predators
    c. Clear brush and unwanted plants from their
       pastures

15. **What have desert-dwelling goats been seen doing to find food?**
    a. Climbing trees
    b. Digging for underground plant roots
    c. Searching for fish in streams

16. What is an adult male goat called?
   a. Stallion or a boar
   b. Ram or a bull
   c. Buck or a billy goat

17. What is an adult female goat called?
   a. Ewe or a cow
   b. Mare or a sow
   c. Doe or nanny goat

18. Are goats social animals that live in groups?
   a. No, they prefer to live alone
   b. Yes, they enjoy playing with other goats
   c. It depends on the breed of goat

# CHAPTER 21. GORILLA

1. Where do gorillas live?
   a. Amazon rainforest
   b. Central African rainforest
   c. Australian rainforest

2. What is a large male gorilla likely to weigh?
   a. 225 pounds
   b. 450 pounds
   c. 675 pounds

3. About how tall is an adult male gorilla standing up?
   a. Six feet
   b. Four feet
   c. Eight feet

4. What is the color of a gorilla's face?
   a. Red
   b. White
   c. Black

5. What is the name of the older male gorilla that leads a group?
   a. Silverback
   b. Whiteback
   c. Grayback

6. What do gorillas eat?
   a. Plants and insects
   b. Meat
   c. Fish

7. Where do gorillas sleep at night?
   a. In caves
   b. In nests they build on the ground or in trees
   c. Out in the open

8. What is the gestation period for a gorilla?
   a. 4 to 6 months
   b. 8 to 10 months
   c. 12 to 14 months

9. How many offspring does a gorilla typically produce?
   a. One
   b. Two
   c. Three

10. **A gorilla's lifespan in the wild is:**
    a. 20-30 years
    b. 35-40 years
    c. 45-50 years

11. **By nature, gorillas are generally:**
    a. Aggressive
    b. Antisocial
    c. Gentle

12. **What do gorillas use to build their nests?**
    a. Rocks
    b. Mud
    c. Leaves, branches and moss

13. **What is the name of the scientist who studied gorillas?**
    a. Dian Fossey
    b. Jane Goodall
    c. Charles Darwin

14. **How do gorillas protect themselves from threats?**
    a. By running away
    b. By hiding in trees
    c. By roaring and beating their chests

15. **What do adult male gorillas use their long canine teeth for?**
    a. To fight each other for leadership
    b. To eat meat
    c. To attract mates

16. A family group of gorillas is called:
   a. A troop
   b. A herd
   c. A flock

17. With whom do young gorillas typically sleep?
   a. Alone
   b. With other young gorillas
   c. With their mothers

18. At what age do gorilla babies begin to hang onto their mothers?
   a. A few weeks old
   b. A few days old
   c. A few hours old

19. For how long do gorilla babies typically continue to hang onto their mothers?
   a. For the first few months
   b. For the first three years
   c. For the first year

CHAPTER 22. HAMSTER

1. The best-known species of hamsters are:
   a. Turkish hamster and Romanian hamster
   b. Chinese hamster and European hamster
   c. Golden hamster and common hamster

2. The golden hamster is also known as the:
   a. Syrian hamster
   b. Black-bellied hamster
   c. Dwarf hamster

3. Hamsters carry food in large pouches located in their:
   a. Cheeks
   b. Stomach
   c. Lungs

4. **What is the average length of a golden hamster?**
   a. Four inches
   b. Eleven inches
   c. Seven inches

5. **What is the average weight of a common hamster?**
   a. Four ounces
   b. Two pounds
   c. Four pounds

6. **What is the gestation period for a golden hamster?**
   a. 24 days
   b. 20 days
   c. 16 days

7. **How many young does a hamster typically give birth to?**
   a. Two to three
   b. Six to seven
   c. Eight to ten

8. **How often does a wild female hamster typically give birth?**
   a. Once a month
   b. Twice a year
   c. Once a year

9. **How long are newborn hamsters typically
   cared for by their mother?**
    a. Three weeks
    b. Six weeks
    c. Eight weeks

10. **What material should be used to line the floor
    of a hamster cage?**
    a. Paper or cardboard
    b. Wood shavings or dried grass
    c. Cloth or fabric

11. **What types of food can pet hamsters be fed?**
    a. Fruits, greens and raw vegetables
    b. Meat and dairy products
    c. Processed foods and sugary treats

12. **Are golden and common hamsters social
    animals?**
    a. Yes
    b. It depends on the species
    c. No

13. **When are hamsters most active?**
    a. During the day
    b. Equally active during the day and night
    c. During the night

14. **What is the typical color of a common
    hamster's underside?**
    a. Brown
    b. Black
    c. White

15. **What is the typical color of a golden hamster's underside?**
   a. White
   b. Black
   c. Brown

16. **What is the typical length of a golden hamster's tail?**
   a. Two inches
   b. One-half inch
   c. Three inches

17. **What is the typical weight of a golden hamster?**
   a. Four ounces
   b. Eight ounces
   c. Twelve ounces

18. **How long do pet hamsters typically live?**
   a. One to two years
   b. Five to six years
   c. Three to four years

CHAPTER 23. HIPPOPOTAMUS (or HIPPO)

1. Where do hippos live?
    a. In the northern parts of Africa
    b. In the middle and southern parts of Africa
    c. In Asia

2. What is the main difference between river hippos and pygmy hippos?
    a. River hippos are larger than pygmy hippos.
    b. River hippos live in water, while pygmy hippos live on land
    c. River hippos are more social than pygmy hippos

3. What is the color of the river hippo's skin?
    a. Brownish-gray
    b. Green
    c. Black

4. What is the shape of a river hippo's body?
   a. Torpedo-shaped
   b. Pear-shaped
   c. Barrel-shaped

5. How many toes does a river hippo have on each foot?
   a. Two
   b. Six
   c. Four

6. Where are the eyes, ears, and nostrils of a hippo located?
   a. Low on its head
   b. High on its head
   c. In the middle of its head

7. How much does a full-grown river hippo usually weigh?
   a. 1,000 to 1,500 pounds
   b. 2,500 to 3,000 pounds
   c. 4,000 to 4,500 pounds

8. About how tall does a full-grown river hippo stand?
   a. Five feet
   b. Three feet
   c. Seven feet

9. **How long is a river hippo, not including the tail?**
   a. 8 to 10 feet
   b. 18 to 20 feet
   c. 12 to 15 feet

10. **How many hippos are usually in a herd?**
    a. 5 to 30
    b. 1 to 5
    c. 30 to 50

11. **What do hippos like to eat?**
    a. Meat
    b. Insects
    c. Water plants

12. **How much food does a river hippo eat in a day?**
    a. 50 pounds
    b. 130 pounds
    c. 200 pounds

13. **What is a baby hippo called?**
    a. Foal
    b. Calf
    c. Cub

14. **What color is the pygmy hippo's skin?**
    a. Blackish
    b. Brownish-gray
    c. White

15. **How much does a full-grown pygmy hippo weigh?**
    a. 400 to 600 pounds
    b. 100 to 200 pounds
    c. 800 to 1,000 pounds

16. **About how tall does a full-grown pygmy hippo stand?**
    a. One foot
    b. Four feet
    c. Two and a half feet

17. **Do pygmy hippos live alone or in herds?**
    a. Both alone and in herds
    b. In herds
    c. Alone or in pairs

18. **How does the head of a pygmy hippo differ from the head of a river hippo?**
    a. The pygmy hippo has a larger head relative to its body size
    b. The pygmy hippo has a smaller head relative to its body size
    c. The pygmy hippo has a different-shaped head

CHAPTER 24. HORSE

1. Horses were domesticated for the first time about how many years ago?
    a. 10,000 years
    b. 5,000 years
    c. 15,000 years

2. What is the tallest, strongest and heaviest type of horse?
    a. Thoroughbred
    b. Racehorse
    c. Draft horse

3. What is the smallest type of horse?
    a. Arabian horse
    b. Quarter horse
    c. Pony

4. What are wild horses that roam free in parts of the Western United States called?
   a. Mustangs
   b. Pintos
   c. Palominos

5. What is the name for a male horse?
   a. Mare
   b. Foal
   c. Stallion

6. What is the name for a female horse?
   a. Stallion
   b. Mare
   c. Foal

7. The gestation period of horses is:
   a. 11 months
   b. 10 months
   c. 12 months

8. What is the term for a newborn horse?
   a. Mare
   b. Foal
   c. Colt

9. How soon after birth can a horse walk and run?
   a. A few hours
   b. A few weeks
   c. A few months

10. How do horses sleep?
   a. They don't sleep
   b. Lying down
   c. Standing up

11. What is the term for a young female horse?
   a. Filly
   b. Colt
   c. Mare

12. What is the name for a young male horse?
   a. Colt
   b. Filly
   c. Mare

13. What is a castrated horse called?
   a. Gelding
   b. Mare
   c. Stallion

14. What do horses eat?
   a. Meat
   b. Grass and other plants
   c. Fish

15. What is the name for a group of wild horses?
   a. Flock
   b. Pack
   c. Herd

16. What are some Olympic sports that involve horses?
   a. Polo
   b. Show jumping, cross-country and dressage
   c. Track and field

17. What is the average lifespan of a horse?
   a. 10 to 20 years
   b. 30 to 40 years
   c. 20 to 30 years

CHAPTER 25. KANGAROO

1. What type of mammal is a kangaroo?
    a. Rodent
    b. Marsupial
    c. Primate

2. Where do kangaroos live?
    a. Mainly in South America
    b. Mainly in North America
    c. Mainly in Australia

3. What are the two main kinds of kangaroos?
    a. Red kangaroos and blue kangaroos
    b. Red kangaroos and gray kangaroos
    c. Gray kangaroos and yellow kangaroos

4. How fast can kangaroos hop?
   a. As fast as 10 miles per hour
   b. As fast as 20 miles per hour
   c. As fast as 30 miles per hour

5. How far can a kangaroo hop?
   a. Up to 40 feet
   b. Up to 30 feet
   c. Up to 20 feet

6. What do kangaroos eat?
   a. Grass and small plants
   b. Meat
   c. Fish

7. How long does a baby kangaroo stay in its mother's pouch?
   a. About six to eight months
   b. About one to two months
   c. About one year

8. What is a baby kangaroo called?
   a. A cub
   b. A kid
   c. A joey

9. Do all kangaroos have pouches?
   a. No, only females have pouches
   b. Yes
   c. Depends on the species

10. **What is a group of kangaroos called?**
    a. A herd
    b. A mob
    c. A pack

11. **Why do kangaroos lick their arms?**
    a. To clean themselves
    b. To eat insects
    c. To cool off

12. **Which of these are not terms for a male and female kangaroo, respectively?**
    a. Buck, doe
    b. Bull, cow
    c. Boomer, flyer

13. **What are kangaroos' hind legs adapted for?**
    a. Hopping and jumping
    b. Running
    c. Climbing

14. **What do kangaroos use their long tails for?**
    a. For balance when hopping
    b. For swimming
    c. For communication

15. **What is the only animal that preys on kangaroos?**
    a. Bears
    b. Lions
    c. Dingoes

16. Are kangaroos protected by law?
   a. No
   b. Yes
   c. Only in certain countries

17. How long do kangaroos usually live?
   a. Two to four years
   b. Six to eight
   c. Ten to twelve years

CHAPTER 26. LION

1. Where do most lions live?
   a. Asia
   b. Africa
   c. Europe

2. What type of habitat do lions prefer?
   a. Savannas
   b. Mountains
   c. Forests

3. What is the average length of an adult male lion?
   a. Six feet
   b. Nine feet
   c. Twelve feet

4. What is the weight of an adult male lion?
   a. 300 pounds
   b. 800 pounds
   c. 560 pounds

5. What is the mane of a male lion made up of?
   a. Long, thick hair
   b. Short, thin hair
   c. Fur

6. What is a female lion called?
   a. She-lion
   b. Queen
   c. Lioness

7. What is the color of a lion's fur?
   a. Brownish-yellow
   b. Black
   c. Gray

8. What is the primary prey of lions?
   a. Rodents
   b. Antelope, buffalo and zebras
   c. Birds

9. What is a group of lions called?
   a. A pack
   b. A herd
   c. A pride

10. At what age do female lions have their first cubs?
   a. One to two years old
   b. Five to six years old
   c. Three to four years old

11. At what age do lion cubs start eating meat?
   a. Six months
   b. Six weeks
   c. Three months

12. What do lion cubs eat for the first six weeks of their lives?
   a. Their mother's milk
   b. Grass
   c. Meat

13. At what age can lion cubs hunt for themselves?
   a. Two years old
   b. One year old
   c. Six months old

14. How do lions spend most of their day?
   a. Eating
   b. Sleeping or resting
   c. Hunting

15. What part of a lion's body gives it the strength to clutch prey and pull it to the ground?
   a. Its jaws
   b. Its claws
   c. Its shoulders and forelegs

16. Which lions do most of the hunting?
   a. The adult males
   b. The adult females
   c. The young lions

17. Why have lions become rare in many parts of Africa?
   a. Hunting
   b. Habitat loss
   c. Disease

18. What is one reason why people kill lions?
   a. To keep them as pets
   b. To sell their fur
   c. To protect livestock

CHAPTER 27. LLAMA

1. How tall is a llama at the shoulder?
    a. Two feet
    b. Three feet
    c. Four feet

2. What is a baby llama called?
    a. Cria
    b. Foal
    c. Cub

3. What is the main use of llamas to people?
    a. As pets
    b. As racing animals
    c. As pack animals

4. How much weight can a llama usually carry?
   a. 50 pounds
   b. 130 pounds
   c. 100 pounds

5. How far can a llama travel in a day with a full load?
   a. 5 to 10 miles
   b. 10 to 15 miles
   c. 15 to 20 miles

6. What will a llama do if it feels its pack is too heavy or if it thinks it has worked hard enough?
   a. Stand still
   b. Run away
   c. Lie down and refuse to move

7. What does a llama do when it is angry or under attack?
   a. Runs away
   b. Spits bad-smelling saliva in its enemy's face
   c. Kicks its attacker

8. What do Native Americans of South America use the hair of the llama for?
   a. To make jewelry
   b. To make garments
   c. To make pottery

9. **What do Native Americans of South America use the hide of the llama for?**
    a. To make sandals
    b. To make hats
    c. To make blankets

10. **What do llamas eat?**
    a. Grasses and low shrubs
    b. Meat
    c. Fruits and vegetables

11. **How much water does a llama need to drink?**
    a. A lot
    b. Not much
    c. None

12. **At the bottom of a llama's feet are:**
    a. Soft pads
    b. Webbed toes
    c. Sticky hairs

13. **How many stomach compartments do llamas have?**
    a. Three
    b. Two
    c. Four

14. **What is the most common noise that llamas make?**
    a. Roar
    b. Bark
    c. Hum

15. What is the average weight of an adult llama?
　　a. 300 to 400 lbs.
　　b. 100 to 200 lbs.
　　c. 500 to 600 lbs.

16. What is a group of llamas called?
　　a. Flock
　　b. Herd
　　c. Pack

17. What is the lifespan of a llama in the wild?
　　a. 5 to 10 years
　　b. 15 to 25 years
　　c. 30 to 35 years

CHAPTER 28. MONKEY

1. Which of the following is *not* a type of monkey?
   a. Chimpanzee
   b. Macaque
   c. Baboon

2. Are monkeys social animals?
   a. No
   b. Yes
   c. Sometimes

3. The largest monkeys, not counting the tail, reach up to:
   a. 32 inches long
   b. 12 inches long
   c. 50 inches long

4. The smallest monkeys, not counting the tail, are less than:
   a. 10 inches long
   b. 6 inches long
   c. 15 inches long

5. What are the world's largest and smallest monkeys, respectively?
   a. Mandrill, pygmy marmoset
   b. Gelada monkey, cotton-top tamarin
   c. Yellow baboon, gray langur

6. How do monkeys form social bonds with each other?
   a. By eating together
   b. To wrestling with each other
   c. By grooming each other

7. Are apes generally smarter than monkeys?
   a. Yes
   b. No
   c. They are of about the same intelligence

8. What is the term for a group of monkeys?
   a. Family
   b. Herd
   c. Troop

9. Which of the following continents is *not* home to monkeys?
   a. Africa
   b. Asia
   c. Europe

10. **What is the most common habitat for monkeys?**
    a. Cold, dry forests
    b. Warm, wet forests
    c. Mountains

11. **What is the primary reason for monkeys having long arms and legs?**
    a. To help them climb trees
    b. To help them dig for food
    c. To help them fight off predators

12. **What do monkeys eat?**
    a. Meat only
    b. Plants only
    c. A variety of plants and animals

13. **Which of these predators is most likely to prey on monkeys?**
    a. Wolves, bears and coyotes
    b. Cheetahs, eagles and hyenas
    c. Snakes, owls and foxes

14. **What is a main difference between monkeys and apes?**
    a. Apes can use simple tools, but monkeys cannot
    b. Apes are part of the human family tree, but monkeys are not
    c. Monkeys have tails, but apes do not

15. **Do monkeys have unique fingerprints like humans?**
    a. No
    b. Yes
    c. Depends on the species

16. **What is a "whistle scream"?**
    a. A unique vocalization of some monkeys that can be heard up to two miles away
    b. A type of monkey dance
    c. A type of monkey food

17. **Which of the following is *not* a reason why many kinds of monkeys are in danger of dying out?**
    a. Destruction of forests and other habitat
    b. Hunting and killing by humans
    c. Overpopulation of monkeys

CHAPTER 29. MOUSE

1. What is the most common type of mouse?
   a. Wood mouse
   b. Field mouse
   c. House mouse

2. A mouse can squeeze through a hole as small as:
   a. 0.25 inches
   b. 0.75 inches
   c. 1.5 inches

3. What do mice eat?
   a. Only insects
   b. Only plant matter
   c. A variety of insects and plant matter

4. What is the average body length of a house mouse, not counting the tail?
   a. One to two inches
   b. Five to six inches
   c. Three to four inches

5. What is the most common color of a house mouse?
   a. Brownish-gray
   b. Black
   c. White

6. In what way are mice useful to people?
   a. They are good companions
   b. They are used to test new medicines and study disease
   c. They are good for pest control

7. What is the average number of times a mouse eats in a day?
   a. 10
   b. 15 to 20
   c. 25

8. At what age can female mice have babies?
   a. One year
   b. Two months
   c. Six months

9. **Up to how many babies can a female mouse have every three weeks?**
   a. 12
   b. 6
   c. 18

10. **How high can mice jump in the air?**
   a. About 6 inches
   b. About 12 inches
   c. About 18 inches

11. **What is the primary reason mice enter homes?**
   a. To find mates
   b. To escape predators
   c. To get out of the cold and find food and water

12. **Do mice hibernate during the winter?**
   a. Yes
   b. No
   c. Only in certain regions

13. **Do mice eat cheese?**
   a. Yes, but their love for it is exaggerated
   b. No
   c. Yes, they love it

14. **Which of the following is a common predator of mice?**
   a. Dogs
   b. Cats
   c. Rabbits

15. A group of mice is known as a:
   a. Herd
   b. Flock
   c. Nest

16. When do a mouse's teeth stop growing?
   a. Never, but constant gnawing on hard surfaces
      keep them at the proper length
   b. After one month
   c. After one year

17. What is the average lifespan of a mouse?
   a. About five years
   b. About two years
   c. About nine years

CHAPTER 30. OCTOPUS

1. An octopus is characterized by:
   a. A rounded body and eight arms
   b. Six arms
   c. A hard external shell

2. Where do the best-known species of octopuses inhabit?
   a. At the bottom of deep parts of the ocean
   b. Near the surface of the ocean
   c. At the bottom of shallow parts of the ocean

3. What is the largest species of octopus called?
   a. South Pacific giant octopus
   b. North Pacific giant octopus
   c. Atlantic giant octopus

4. **How do octopuses breathe?**
    a. By filtering oxygen out of the water through gills
    b. Through their skin
    c. By inhaling air from the surface

5. **What is the octopus's main heart responsible for?**
    a. Supplying blood to the tentacles
    b. Pumping blood throughout the body
    c. Regulating blood pressure

6. **What are the octopus's two smaller, peripheral hearts responsible for?**
    a. Supplying blood to the gills
    b. Regulating body temperature
    c. Supplying blood to the brain

7. **How many eyes does an octopus have?**
    a. Four
    b. Six
    c. Two

8. **What do octopuses primarily feed on?**
    a. Seaweed
    b. Clams, crabs and snails
    c. Plankton

9. **Which is *not* a means by which octopuses capture their prey?**
    a. Wrapping them in the webbing between their arms
    b. Creating an electric field
    c. Injecting toxin into them

10. Which is *not* a means by which octopuses
    avoid predators?
    a. Releasing a high-pitched sound
    b. Discharging a cloud of inky fluid
    c. Quickly swimming backwards

11. How many eggs can females of some octopus
    species lay?
    a. More than 10,000
    b. Less than 1,000
    c. More than 100,000

12. What happens to baby octopuses after they
    hatch?
    a. They swim at or near the surface of the water
       for several weeks
    b. They immediately descend to the ocean bottom
    c. They are cared for by their mother

13. What is the unique feature of the small blue
    ringed octopuses of Australia?
    a. They reproduce asexually
    b. They have a venom that can kill people
    c. They can change their size at will

14. Can an octopus regrow a lost arm?
    a. Depends on the species
    b. No
    c. Yes

15. What is the primary group of animals to which octopuses belong?
a. Fish
b. Mollusks
c. Crustaceans

16. What is the main method of locomotion for an octopus?
a. Floating with sea currents
b. Using its arms and suckers to move along the ocean bottom
c. Swimming using fins

17. How long do most octopuses live?
a. More than five years
b. More than ten years
c. One to three years

CHAPTER 31. OSTRICH

1. Where do wild ostriches live?
   a. The mountains of Asia
   b. The forests of South America
   c. The plains and deserts of Africa

2. How tall can an ostrich be?
   a. Six feet
   b. Seven feet
   c. Eight feet

3. How much can ostriches weigh?
   a. Up to 220 pounds
   b. Up to 345 pounds
   c. Up to 150 pounds

4. How fast can an ostrich run?
    a. More than 40 miles per hour
    b. More than 20 miles per hour
    c. More than 30 miles per hour

5. What color are the feathers on a male ostrich's body?
    a. Black
    b. Brown
    c. White

6. What color are the feathers on a male ostrich's wings and tail?
    a. Black
    b. Brown
    c. White

7. What color are the feathers on a female ostrich?
    a. White
    b. Black
    c. Brown

8. Can an ostrich fly?
    a. Yes
    b. Only short distances
    c. No

9. What is the mainstay of an ostrich's diet?
    a. Plants
    b. Insects
    c. Small animals

10. An ostrich's eyelashes are:
   a. Short and yellow
   b. Thick and black
   c. Long and white

11. How can an ostrich kill a lion?
   a. By smothering it
   b. By kicking it
   c. By injecting a toxin

12. How many toes does an ostrich have on each foot?
   a. Two
   b. Three
   c. Four

13. What can ostriches use their thick nails for?
   a. Digging nests
   b. Climbing trees
   c. Defending themselves against predators

14. What helps ostriches escape from predators?
   a. Their speed and good eyesight
   b. Their ability to hide in the sand
   c. Their thick and strong feathers

15. How long can ostriches live without drinking if they eat moist plants?
   a. For more than two weeks
   b. For a few days
   c. For a week

16. How many eggs can one female ostrich lay in a nest?
    a. Up to five
    b. Up to ten
    c. Up to two

17. Who sits on the eggs to keep them warm?
    a. Male ostrich during the day, female during the
       night
    b. Female ostrich during the day, male during the
       night
    c. Female ostrich during both day and night

**18. Is it true that ostriches bury their heads in the
    sand?**
    a. No, but they lower their heads to the ground to
       blend in with their surroundings
    b. Yes
    c. Only the females

19. How long can ostriches live?
    a. Up to 60 years
    b. Up to 70 years
    c. Up to 50 years

CHAPTER 32. OWL

1. What is the smallest kind of owl, with a body size of only about five inches?
   a. Elf owl
   b. Northern pygmy owl
   c. Eastern screech owl

2. What is the largest kind of owl, with a body size as long as 33 inches?
   a. Great gray owl
   b. Spotted owl
   c. Barn owl

3. What does an owl's collar of feathers do?
   a. It protects the owl's head from predators
   b. It helps the owl camouflage itself
   c. It reflects sound to the owl's ears

4. An owl's eyes are:
  a. Capable of seeing in total darkness
  b. Located on the sides of its head, providing a
     wide field of view
  c. Tube-shaped, forward-looking and immobile

5. An owl can rotate its neck as much as:
  a. 180 degrees
  b. 270 degrees
  c. 90 degrees

6. What are owl pellets?
  a. Droppings (excrement)
  b. Disk-shaped food for pet owls
  c. Balls of coughed-up bones and fur that the owl
     cannot digest

7. What is the owl a traditional symbol of?
  a. Wisdom
  b. Strength
  c. Beauty

8. What is the body of an owl like?
  a. Long and thin
  b. Short and thick
  c. Round and fluffy

9. What kind of beak does an owl have?
  a. Short and straight
  b. Short and hooked
  c. Long and curved

10. What are most owls' feathers like?
   a. Long and soft
   b. Short and stiff
   c. Small and round

11. What color are most owls' feathers?
   a. Bright and colorful
   b. White and black
   c. Dull and dark

12. Owls eat mostly:
   a. Plant tissue
   b. Small mammals
   c. Insects and worms

13. What does an owl do with small pieces of food?
   a. It swallows it whole
   b. It chews it normally
   c. It rejects it by dropping it on the ground

14. How many eggs do most female owls lay?
   a. One
   b. Twelve
   c. Three to four

15. Do both male and female owls help care for the eggs and young?
   a. Depends on the species
   b. No
   c. Yes

16. A group of owls is known as a:
   a. Parliament
   b. Host
   c. Brood

17. When do owls typically hunt?
   a. During the day
   b. At night
   c. During the twilight hours of dawn and dusk

CHAPTER 33. PANDA (GIANT PANDA)

1. Which of the following is *not* a common name for the giant panda?
  a. Panda bear
  b. Raccoon panda
  c. Panda

2. How much bamboo can a giant panda eat in a day?
  a. 35 pounds
  b. 55 pounds
  c. 85 pounds

3. Which parts of the bamboo plant do pandas *not* eat?
  a. Leaves and stems
  b. Tough outer layers of shoots
  c. Soft inner tissue of shoots

4. **What is the distinguishing feature that allows giant pandas to grasp bamboo?**
   a. A true opposable thumb
   b. An "extra thumb" that grows from the wrist of each front paw
   c. Fingers

5. **What is the primary reason giant pandas are in danger of dying out?**
   a. Disease
   b. Predator attack
   c. Habitat loss

6. **How many cubs do female pandas typically give birth to in each delivery?**
   a. One to two
   b. Three to four
   c. Five to six

7. **What is the approximate weight of a newborn giant panda cub?**
   a. One pound
   b. Five ounces
   c. Five pounds

8. **For how long do giant panda cubs typically nurse?**
   a. One year
   b. Six months
   c. Two years

9. What is the goal of zoos breeding giant
   pandas?
      a. To supply giant pandas to zoos around the
         world
      b. To study giant panda behavior
      c. To increase the population of giant pandas

10. What is the current classification of giant
    pandas?
       a. Members of the bear family
       b. Members of the large cat family
       c. Members of the raccoon family

11. What is the approximate length of an adult
    giant panda?
       a. Nine to ten feet
       b. Seven to eight feet
       c. Five to six feet

12. What is the approximate weight of an adult
    giant panda?
       a. 200 to 300 pounds
       b. 300 to 400 pounds
       c. 400 to 500 pounds

13. What is the color of a giant panda's body?
       a. Black and white
       b. White
       c. Brown and white

14. **What is the color of a giant panda's legs?**
    a. Black
    b. White
    c. Brown

15. **Where are giant pandas found in the wild?**
    a. Northeast China
    b. Central China
    c. Southeast China

16. **What do we call a group of pandas?**
    a. A mischief
    b. A congress
    c. An embarrassment

17. **What bamboo-eating, raccoonlike mammal, which is smaller than the giant panda, contains the word "panda" in its name even though it is not related to the giant panda?**
    a. The white panda
    b. The brown panda
    c. The red panda

CHAPTER 34. PARROT

1. Parrots are found in which of these regions?
    a. Central America, South America and Australia
    b. Europe, Asia and Africa
    c. North America, South America and Europe

2. Which of these is *not* a physical characteristic of parrots?
    a. They have long legs and a short tail
    b. Their feet have two toes pointing forward and two pointing backward
    c. They have a thick, hooked beak

3. What allows parrots to mimic human speech?
    a. Unique vocal cords
    b. A strong, hooked beak
    c. A larynx-like structure, called the syrinx, located near the windpipe

4. What is the term for a young parrot?
   a. Chick
   b. Fledgling
   c. Nestling

5. What is the term for an adult male parrot?
   a. Rooster
   b. Cock
   c. Drake

6. How many newborn parrots does a female parrot typically lay?
   a. One to two
   b. Four to six
   c. Two to four

7. Female parrots lay eggs that are:
   a. Blue and oval-shaped
   b. White and round
   c. Brown and tapered at one end

8. How tall are the largest parrots?
   a. More than one foot
   b. More than three feet
   c. More than two feet

9. How tall are the smallest parrots?
   a. About seven inches
   b. About five inches
   c. About three inches

10. What are some predators of parrots?
   a. Mice, rats and squirrels
   b. Lions, tigers and bears
   c. Jaguars, hawks and snakes

**11. Which of these is *not* typically part of a
   parrot's diet?**
   a. Fruits and nuts
   b. Seeds and buds
   c. Small animals

12. In what type of habitat do most parrots live?
   a. Mountains
   b. Rainforests
   c. Swampland

**13. When not hunting for food, parrots spend
   most of their time:**
   a. Grooming themselves
   b. Resting
   c. Vocalizing

14. Are parrots social creatures?
   a. No; they tend to live alone
   b. Yes; they tend to live in groups
   c. Somewhat; they tend to live in pairs

15. The world's only flightless parrot is:
   a. The kakapo of New Zealand
   b. The cockatoo of Australia
   c. The macaw of South America

16. Which of these is *not* a term for a group of
    parrots?
    a. Brood
    b. Company
    c. Pandemonium

17. What is the approximate lifespan of a parrot?
    a. 20 to 30 years
    b. 40 to 50 years
    c. 60 to 70 years

CHAPTER 35. PEACOCK (PEAFOWL)

Note: Although people often use the term *peacock* to refer to both sexes, technically the term refers to only the male. The female is known as a *peahen* and the baby is a *peachick*. The collective term for both males and females is *peafowl*.

1. What is the natural habitat of peafowl?
   a. Mountains
   b. Deserts
   c. Forests and rainforests

2. What is the term for the large colorful "tail" of a peacock?
   a. Plumage
   b. Feathers
   c. Train

3. How big is a male peacock?
   a. About the size of a turkey
   b. About the size of a chicken
   c. About the size of a ostrich

4. What color is the male peacock's neck and breast?
   a. Brown
   b. Blue
   c. Green

5. What color is the male peacock's back?
   a. Blue
   b. Brown
   c. Green

6. What is a typical color of a peahen?
   a. Metallic green
   b. Vivid blue
   c. Dull tan or brown

7. What is a common feature of all peafowl?
   a. Bare patches of skin around their eyes
   b. Long, slender necks
   c. Short, thick legs

8. How fast can peacocks run?
   a. 10 miles per hour
   b. 5 miles per hour
   c. 15 miles per hour

9. **What do all species of peafowl have on top of
   their heads?**
   a. Combs
   b. Horns
   c. Crests

10. **How do peafowl prefer to live?**
    a. Alone
    b. In small groups
    c. In large flocks

11. **How often do peacocks shed their feathers?**
    a. Once a year
    b. Every two years
    c. Never

12. **What does a peacock do to impress a peahen
    during breeding season?**
    a. Build a nest
    b. Display his colorful feathers
    c. Sing a song

13. **How long have peacocks been kept in
    captivity?**
    a. For more than 1,000 years
    b. For more than 2,000 years
    c. For more than 500 years

14. **How many eggs can a peahen lay at a time?**
    a. Up to six
    b. Up to four
    c. Up to two

15. Where does the peahen make her nest?
   a. In a tree
   b. In a protected spot on the ground.
   c. In a burrow

16. Which is *not* part of the peafowl's diet?
   a. A variety of plants and insects
   b. A variety of certain reptiles and amphibians
   c. A variety of fish

17. How large is the wingspan of a peacock?
   a. About three feet
   b. About five feet
   c. About seven feet

18. Why are the feathers of a peacock covered in tiny crystals?
   a. To protect them from the sun
   b. To help them fly
   c. To play a large part in attracting the females.

19. How long can peafowl live in captivity?
   a. Up to 20 years
   b. Up to 50 years
   c. Up to 10 years

CHAPTER 36. PENGUIN

1. Wild penguins live:
   a. In the northern hemisphere
   b. In the southern hemisphere
   c. On islands near the North Pole

2. Thousands of penguins may nest in the same area. These groups are called:
   a. Families
   b. Colonies
   c. Flocks

3. Adult penguins are covered with feathers that are:
   a. Long and thin
   b. Fluffy
   c. Short and thick

4. **Penguins use their wings for:**
   a. Flying
   b. Communicating
   c. Swimming

5. **The back, head, and wing feathers of penguins are:**
   a. White
   b. Black or bluish-gray
   c. Dark blue

6. **Penguins eat mostly:**
   a. Fish, crabs and shrimp
   b. Sea plants
   c. Plankton

7. **Over many generations, the wings of penguins:**
   a. Took the shape of flippers
   b. Got smaller
   c. Got larger

8. **Penguins get drinking water by:**
   a. Drinking seawater directly
   b. Eating snow
   c. Obtaining water from plants

9. **How do male penguins keep their mate's eggs warm in cold places?**
   a. By building nests out of twigs and leaves
   b. By balancing their eggs on their feet and
      covering them with belly flap
   c. By burying the eggs in the ground

10. When does a penguin chick first start communicating with its parents?
a. Immediately after hatching
b. About two days after hatching
c. About a week after hatching

11. What is the main mode of transportation for penguins?
a. Swimming
b. Flying
c. Walking

12. How do penguins sleep?
a. Standing up
b. Lying down
c. Lying down or standing up

13. How do penguins stay warm in cold environments?
a. They grow additional feathers
b. They remain in the water
c. They huddle together

14. How high can penguins jump out of the water?
a. About three feet
b. About six feet
c. About ten feet

15. What is the average swimming speed of most
    penguin species?
    a. About 5 miles per hour
    b. About 10 miles per hour
    c. About 15 miles per hour

16. What percent of a penguin's life is spent in the
    water?
    a. About 75 percent
    b. About 50 percent
    c. About 25 percent

17. How long does a penguin typically live?
    a. Less than 10 years
    b. More than 30 years
    c. Between 15 and 20 years

CHAPTER 37. PIG

1. Pigs are *not* native to:
   a. Africa
   b. Europe and Asia
   c. North and South America

2. Where do wild pigs *not* typically live?
   a. Forests
   b. Mountains
   c. Grasslands

3. Based on their food consumption, pigs are classified as:
   a. Carnivores (meat eaters)
   b. Omnivores (meat and plant eaters)
   c. Herbivores (plant eaters)

4. **Which country has the most domestic pigs?**
   a. China
   b. India
   c. United States

5. **What is the name for both wild and domestic pigs?**
   a. Boars
   b. Swine
   c. Hogs

6. **What is another name for a domestic pig that weighs more than 120 pounds?**
   a. Boar
   b. Hog
   c. Porker

7. **What does a pig use its snout for?**
   a. Vocal communication
   b. Grabbing and holding objects
   c. Finding food in the ground and digging it out

8. **Do pigs have tusks?**
   a. Wild pigs do, but domestic pigs don't
   b. No; pigs do not have tusks
   c. Yes; all pigs have tusks

9. **What is the main use for the hide of a domestic pig?**
   a. To make leather
   b. To make shoes
   c. To make furniture upholstery

10. Which food products do *not* come from the
pig?
  a. Tofu and yogurt
  b. Lard and gelatin
  c. Pork chops and bacon

11. What is the stiff hair of pigs used for?
  a. Medical devises
  b. Brush bristles
  c. Electronic manufacturing

12. In the wild, a group of female pigs and their
young is known as a:
  a. Passel
  b. Drove
  c. Sounder

13. Which is *not* a reason for pigs to roll around in
the mud?
  a. They need to cool off (because they have no
     sweat glands)
  b. They need to protect their skin from the sun
     and from biting insects
  c. They are naturally dirty animals

14. Why are pigs often used in medical research?
  a. They share many anatomical similarities with
     humans
  b. They are easy to care for
  c. They are readily available and inexpensive

**15. Which is *not* something pigs are trained to
detect with their noses?**
a. Truffles
b. Cancer and other diseases in humans
c. Dangerous chemicals

16. How long is the average pregnancy for a pig?
a. Eight months
b. Six months
c. Four months

17. What is the average litter size for pigs?
a. 4 to 5 piglets
b. 10 to 11 piglets
c. 15 to 20 piglets

18. How long can wild pigs live?
a. Up to 25 years or more
b. 8 to 12 years
c. 15 to 20 years

CHAPTER 38. PLATYPUS

1. A platypus is:
    a. A waterfowl
    b. A semi-aquatic reptile
    c. An egg-laying mammal

2. A platypus's body is covered with:
    a. Scales
    b. Feathers
    c. Fur

3. Where does the platypus live?
    a. Near rivers and streams in eastern Australia
    b. In the forests of New Guinea
    c. On the islands of Tasmania

4. **Which does *not* aid in the platypus's swimming?**
   a. Its webbed feet
   b. Its snout, which looks like a duck's bill
   c. Its broad, flat tail

5. **How long does the platypus typically dive underwater?**
   a. 18 to 40 seconds
   b. 1 to 2 minutes
   c. 5 to 6 minutes

6. **What does the platypus use to detect its prey?**
   a. Its sharp eyesight
   b. Special sensors on its bill that detect electrical currents
   c. Its keen sense of smell

7. **How do adult platypuses crush their food?**
   a. With their teeth
   b. With their strong claws
   c. With horny pads at the back of the jaws

8. **In the banks of streams, platypuses dig burrows that can be as long as:**
   a. 50 feet
   b. 85 feet
   c. 15 feet

**9. How long does a young platypus remain in its
  mother's burrow?**
   a. About six months
   b. About four months
   c. About one year

**10. How does a young platypus feed in its
   mother's burrow?**
   a. It drinks its mother's milk
   b. It eats solid food brought to it by its mother
   c. It feeds on insects and small invertebrates

**11. What is the primary food source for adult
   platypuses?**
   a. Reptiles and amphibians
   b. Fish and water plants
   c. Worms, shellfish and crustaceans

**12. How many eggs does a female platypus
   typically lay?**
   a. Seven to ten
   b. Four to six
   c. One to three

**13. What is the approximate size of a platypus
   egg?**
   a. About two inches in diameter
   b. About one inch in diameter
   c. About one-half inch in diameter

14. **What is the texture of platypus eggs?**
     a. Soft and pliable
     b. Leathery, similar to reptile eggs
     c. Hard and brittle

15. **Are platypuses social animals?**
     a. No; each adult lives in its own burrow
     b. Somewhat; they live in pairs
     c. Yes; they live in groups

16. **How do platypuses swim and steer?**
     a. Swim with back feet, steer with front feet
     b. Swim with front feet, steer with back feet
     c. Swim with front and back feet, steer with tail

17. **How much sleep do platypuses typically get each day?**
     a. About 10 hours
     b. About 14 hours
     c. About 6 hours

18. **Why were platypuses hunted in the past?**
     a. For their fur
     b. For their meat
     c. For sport

19. **In captivity platypuses can live as long as about:**
     a. 17 years
     b. 10 years
     c. 25 years

CHAPTER 39. RABBIT

1. Rabbits were once considered to be rodents; they no longer are because:
   a. They are social creatures
   b. They have four upper incisor teeth rather than two
   c. They eat plants

2. About how many known breeds of rabbits are there?
   a. 55
   b. 35
   c. 45

3. What is the largest breed of domestic rabbit?
   a. Flemish Giant
   b. Checkered Giant
   c. Hungarian Giant

4. **What is the smallest breed of wild rabbit?**
    a. Teddy Dwarf
    b. Jersey Wooly
    c. Columbia Basin Pygmy

5. **What do rabbits use their strong front teeth for?**
    a. Digging burrows
    b. Chewing plants
    c. Fighting

6. **When do rabbits' teeth stop growing?**
    a. When they reach adulthood
    b. Never
    c. After about three months

7. **Which two senses are very well developed in rabbits?**
    a. Smell and hearing
    b. Smell and taste
    c. Hearing and sight

8. **How do rabbits help keep themselves cool in hot temperatures?**
    a. By drinking water
    b. By sweating
    c. By giving off heat from their ears

9. **Other than as pets, what is one way that people use rabbits?**
    a. As laboratory animals
    b. As circus performers
    c. For pest control

10. **What happened when European settlers brought rabbits to Australia?**
    a. The rabbits became a pest and harmed native wildlife
    b. The rabbits became a popular food source
    c. The rabbits failed to survive

11. **Are pet rabbits usually larger than wild rabbits?**
    a. They are about the same size
    b. No
    c. Yes

12. **What bodily function are rabbits physically incapable of?**
    a. Passing gas
    b. Sneezing
    c. Snoring

13. **What is one way that hay helps rabbits digest their food?**
    a. It prevents the formation of fur balls in their stomachs
    b. It provides essential digestive enzymes
    c. It breaks down the food into smaller particles

14. **How long does a mother rabbit feed her kittens each day?**
    a. About 30 minutes
    b. About five minutes
    c. About an hour

15. What color is raw rabbit meat?
  a. Red
  b. White
  c. Tan

16. At what age do rabbits start breeding?
  a. At about one year
  b. At about six to eight months
  c. As early as three to four months

17. Can a rabbit die of a heart attack if suddenly startled by a predator?
  a. Yes, frequently
  b. Sometimes, but not often
  c. Never

18. How long can a domestic rabbit live if properly cared for?
  a. Up to 15 years
  b. Up to 5 years
  c. Up to 10 years

CHAPTER 40. RACCOON

1. Raccoons are originally from which continent?
    a. Europe
    b. South America
    c. North America

2. Raccoon's are sometimes called "bandits" because:
    a. They steal cat food and dog food
    b. They kill chickens and ducks
    c. They have a black mask of fur surrounding their eyes

3. The raccoon's diet puts it in which category?
    a. Carnivore (meat eater)
    b. Omnivore (meat and plant eater)
    c. Herbivore (plant eater)

4. What is the gestation period of a raccoon?
   a. About 30 days
   b. About 90 days
   c. About 65 days

5. What are raccoon babies called?
   a. Pups
   b. Kits
   c. Cubs

6. Do raccoons hibernate in the winter?
   a. Yes; all raccoons hibernate
   b. No; they migrate to warmer climates
   c. No; they grow thick coats and stay asleep in
      their dens

7. What is the raccoon's most common fur color?
   a. Grayish-brown
   b. White
   c. Black

8. The raccoon's tail color is typically:
   a. Solid black or dark brown
   b. Striped, with alternating yellow and brown rings
   c. Striped, with alternating gray and white rings

9. What is the raccoon's usual activity period?
   a. Daytime
   b. Nighttime
   c. Dusk or dawn

10. Most adult raccoons weigh between:
   a. 10 and 20 pounds
   b. 20 and 30 pounds
   c. 5 and 10 pounds

11. What is the raccoon's average length, including the tail?
   a. One to two feet
   b. Three to four feet
   c. Two to three feet

12. What is the primary social structure of raccoons?
   a. They live alone or in small family groups
   b. They always live alone
   c. They live in large colonies

13. How many different sounds can raccoons make to communicate?
   a. Over fifty
   b. Less than ten
   c. About twenty-five

14. What is a unique feature of a raccoon's front paws?
   a. They become more sensitive when wet
   b. They have opposable thumbs for grasping
   c. They have webbed paws for swimming

15. Which is *not* a term for a group of raccoons?
   a. A gaze
   b. A nursery
   c. A colony

16. How does a raccoon's intelligence compare to that of other mammals?
a. More intelligent
b. About the same
c. Less intelligent

17. How fast can raccoons run?
a. Up to about 20 miles per hour
b. Up to about 15 miles per hour
c. Up to about 30 miles per hour

18. A raccoon in captivity can live up to about:
a. 20 years
b. 10 years
c. 5 years

19. How long do raccoons typically live in the wild?
a. Five to seven years
b. Two to three years
c. Ten to fifteen years

CHAPTER 41. RHINOCEROS (RHINO)

1. In which continents can rhinos be found?
   a. Europe and North America
   b. Africa and Asia
   c. South America and Australia

2. What is the primary diet of a rhinoceros?
   a. Meat and fish
   b. Grass and roots
   c. Fruits and vegetables

3. What is the primary function of horns for rhinos?
   a. To attract mates
   b. To dig for food
   c. As weapons during confrontations and for protection

4. **What is the typical gestation period for a rhinoceros?**
   a. 15 to 17 months
   b. 9 to 12 months
   c. 18 to 24 months

5. **What is the approximate weight of a rhinoceros calf at birth?**
   a. 65 to 100 pounds
   b. 20 to 35 pounds
   c. 110 to 130 pounds

6. **How long do rhinoceros calves typically suckle?**
   a. Up to two years
   b. Up to one year
   c. Up to three years

7. **When do rhinoceros calves typically start developing horns?**
   a. Between one and two months of age
   b. At birth
   c. After one year of age

8. **For how long do rhinoceros calves typically remain with their mothers before becoming independent?**
   a. One to two years
   b. Three to five years
   c. Two to four years

9. When does a rhino's horn stop growing?
   a. After about five years
   b. Never
   c. After about three years

10. What is the main material that rhinoceros horns are made of?
   a. Bone
   b. Ivory
   c. Keratin

11. A rhinoceros can weigh up to about:
   a. 4,400 pounds
   b. 2.200 pounds
   c. 1,100 pounds

12. About how tall can a rhinoceros be?
   a. Four to five feet
   b. Five to six feet
   c. Six to seven feet

13. An adult rhinoceros can be up to about how many feet in length?
   a. Twelve feet
   b. Ten feet
   c. Eight feet

14. How does the rhinoceros protect itself from insects?
   a. By wallowing in mud
   b. By using its thick skin as a shield
   c. By forming symbiotic relationships with
      birds, which remove them

15. **What is the primary reason why rhinos are hunted?**
   a. For their meat
   b. For their skin
   c. For their horns

16. **In what regions are rhinoceros horns used in medicine?**
   a. Africa
   b. Asia
   c. South America

17. **In what countries are rhinoceros horns used to make dagger handles?**
   a. Nigeria and Kenya
   b. China and India
   c. Yemen and Oman

18. **What is the typical lifespan of a rhinoceros in the wild?**
   a. Up to about 45 years
   b. Up to about 30 years
   c. Up to about 15 years

CHAPTER 42. SEAL

1. Seals are aquatic mammals that can be found:
    a. Exclusively in the Arctic and Antarctic oceans
    b. Mainly in the waters of Australia and its surrounding islands
    c. Across the globe, including both open oceans and coastal areas

2. In what environments can seals survive?
    a. Both polar and tropical waters
    b. Only in polar waters
    c. Only in tropical waters

3. Most seals are adapted to live in:
    a. Saltwater habitats, including oceans and seas
    b. Freshwater environments such as lakes and rivers
    c. Both freshwater and saltwater environments with equal ease

4. How much time do most seals spend on land and in water?
   a. Most of their time in water
   b. About half their time on land and half in water
   c. Most of their time on land

5. Seals come ashore to:
   a. Breed or rest
   b. Forage for fruits or berries that grow near the shore
   c. Escape predators

6. Instead of legs and feet, seals have:
   a. Fins
   b. Flippers
   c. A tail

7. How long can seals hold their breath underwater?
   a. Up to 30 minutes
   b. Up to 2 hours
   c. Up to 1 hour

8. How deep can some seals dive?
   a. Deeper than 1,000 yards
   b. Deeper than 500 yards
   c. Deeper than 200 yards

9. The smallest adult seals are about:
   a. One foot long and weigh 50 pounds
   b. Eight feet long and weigh 500 pounds
   c. Four feet long and weigh 200 pounds

10. The largest seals can be as much as:
    a. 12 feet long and weigh 6,000 pounds
    b. 16 feet long and weigh more than 8,000 pounds
    c. 8 feet long and weigh 4,000 pounds

11. Why do some seals migrate hundreds of miles every year?
    a. To search for food
    b. To escape harsh weather conditions
    c. To find new breeding grounds

12. What helps keep seals warm in icy water?
    a. They are warm-blooded animals
    b. They have a dense coat of hair
    c. They have a thick layer of fat, called blubber

13. Seals primarily feed on:
    a. Fish, squid and other marine creatures
    b. Insects and crustaceans
    c. Plants and algae found in aquatic environments

14. Seals communicate through a combination of:
    a. Scent markings and chemical signals
    b. Electrical impulses and touch-sensitive receptors
    c. Vocalizations and body gestures

15. Are seals social animals?
    a. No; they prefer minimal contact with others
    b. Yes; they often form colonies on land or gather in groups in the water
    c. Somewhat; they form territorial groups that defend their home ranges

16. Which is *not* a threat to seal populations?
   a. Fishing nets
   b. Pollution of oceans from plastics and chemical
      waste
   c. Natural predators, such as sharks and killer
      whales

17. How long can seals typically live?
   a. For 10 to 15 years
   b. For 15 to 20 years
   c. For 30 years or more

CHAPTER 43. SHARK

1. How long have sharks existed?
   a. More than 300 million years
   b. Less than 100 million years
   c. Only a few thousand years

2. Where do most sharks live?
   a. In cold Arctic oceans
   b. In mild or warm oceans
   c. In large lakes

3. What do most sharks eat?
   a. Dead or dying animals
   b. Live fish, including other sharks
   c. Plants and algae

4. What is the shape of most sharks?
   a. Flat and wide
   b. Round and plump
   c. Long and torpedo-shaped

5. **What is the skeleton of a shark made of?**
   a. Bone
   b. Ligaments and tendons
   c. Cartilage

6. **Which of the following statements is *not* true of sharks?**
   a. They can detect a single drop of blood in the ocean
   b. They have rows of sharp teeth that are constantly being replaced
   c. They have gills that are located on the underside of their bodies

7. **Which sense best helps sharks find their prey?**
   a. Sight
   b. Smell
   c. Hearing

8. **How fast can most sharks swim?**
   a. 20 to 30 miles per hour
   b. 5 to 10 miles per hour
   c. More than 40 miles per hour

9. **What is the largest kind of shark?**
   a. Tiger shark
   b. Whale shark
   c. Great white shark

10. **Which sharks are considered dangerous to humans?**
    a. All sharks
    b. Only a few species, when they are hungry or disturbed
    c. None

11. **How often do shark attacks on humans occur?**
    a. Frequently
    b. Never
    c. Rarely

12. **Which is the fastest shark?**
    a. Hammerhead shark
    b. Tiger shark
    c. Mako shark

13. **Which shark lives in the deepest parts of the ocean?**
    a. Portuguese shark
    b. Sand shark
    c. Greenland shark

14. **What do young sharks eat when they are born?**
    a. Plankton
    b. Their own teeth
    c. Small fish

15. **What kind of teeth do all sharks have?**
    a. Round teeth
    b. Blunt teeth
    c. Triangular serrated teeth

16. When do many sharks merge with groups?
   a. Only when they are threatened by predators
   b. Only when they are hunting
   c. Only when it is breeding season or for migration

17. A shark's skin feels:
   a. Rough, like sandpaper
   b. Smooth, like silk
   c. Rubbery, like a soccer ball

**18. In which continent are shark fins often used
   to make soup?**
   a. Asia
   b. Australia
   c. Africa

CHAPTER 44. SHEEP

1. Sheep most likely originated in:
   a. Africa
   b. Central Asia
   c. Europe

2. On which continents are sheep found?
   a. All continents except Antarctica and Australia
   b. All continents except Antarctica and Africa
   c. All continents except Antarctica

3. Which is the world's leading sheep-producing country?
   a. Australia
   b. China
   c. New Zealand

4. What is the name of the thick coat of fibers
that sheep grow?
   a. Hair
   b. Fur
   c. Wool

5. How many toes do sheep have on each hoof?
   a. Six
   b. Four
   c. Two

6. Which sex of sheep typically has horns?
   a. Most males and some females
   b. Neither
   c. Males only

7. What is the term for a large sheep farm in
Australia and New Zealand?
   a. Station
   b. Ranch
   c. Homestead

8. What are the terms for a male sheep and
female sheep, respectively?
   a. Stallion, mare
   b. Bull, cow
   c. Ram, ewe

9. What is the term for a young sheep?
   a. Lamb
   b. Calf
   c. Colt

10. **What is the primary food source for sheep?**
   a. Meat
   b. Insects
   c. Grass and plants

11. **How many separate stomach compartments do sheep have?**
   a. Four
   b. Three
   c. Two

12. **What is the meat of an adult sheep called?**
   a. Lamb
   b. Mutton
   c. Veal

13. **What is the meat of a younger sheep called?**
   a. Mutton
   b. Lamb
   c. Veal

14. **What is the term for a group of sheep?**
   a. Flock
   b. Herd
   c. Drove

15. **Where do sheep have teeth?**
   a. In both their upper and lower jaws
   b. Only in their lower jaw
   c. Only in their upper jaw

16. **Which, typically, are predators of sheep?**
    a. Lions and tigers
    b. Wolves and coyotes
    c. Snakes and lizards

17. **What is the approximate lifespan of a sheep in captivity?**
    a. 10 to 12 years
    b. 7 to 9 years
    c. 15 to 20 years

CHAPTER 45. SKUNK

1. Where do most skunks live?
- a. Under fallen logs
- b. In hollow trees
- c. In underground dens

2. On what continents are skunks found?
- a. North America and South America
- b. Europe and Africa
- c. Asia and Australia

3. What is the purpose of a skunk's black and white fur pattern?
- a. It serves as a warning signal to potential predators
- b. It helps them blend in with their surroundings for camouflage
- c. It aids in courtship and mate recognition

4. **What is the purpose of a skunk's musk (the foul-smelling liquid it sprays)?**
   a. To attract mates
   b. To defend itself from predators
   c. To mark territory

5. **Which is *not* a warning sign that a skunk is about to spray?**
   a. It stamps its front feet
   b. It hisses or growls
   c. It raises its tail

6. **How far can a skunk spray its foul-smelling liquid?**
   a. It can only spray a few feet
   b. It can spray over 20 feet
   c. It can spray up to 12 feet

7. **What is the primary target of a skunk's spray?**
   a. It aims for the eyes of its enemy
   b. It aims for the mouth of its enemy
   c. It aims for the nose of its enemy

8. **How long does the odor of skunk musk typically linger?**
   a. A few hours
   b. Two to three weeks
   c. Several days

9. **Can tomato juice neutralize skunk musk?**
   a. No
   b. Yes
   c. Only if applied immediately

10. **How long does it take for a skunk to replenish its spray supply?**
    a. A few hours
    b. Several weeks
    c. 10 to 12 days

11. **What is the typical size of a skunk?**
    a. They are comparable in size to a house cat
    b. They are about the size of a large dog
    c. They are much smaller than a house cat

12. **What is the social structure of skunks?**
    a. They live in large, communal groups
    b. They are solitary animals for most of the year
    c. They form strong bonds with a mate

13. **When are skunks most active?**
    a. They are primarily active during the day
    b. They are equally active at night and during the day
    c. They are primarily active at night

14. **What is the technical classification of skunks?**
    a. Carnivores (meat eaters)
    b. Omnivores (meat and plant eaters)
    c. Herbivores (plant eaters)

15. **Which animals are most likely to attack a skunk?**
    a. Wolves and bears
    b. Snakes and raccoons
    c. Bobcats and owls

**16. How many young does a female skunk
    typically give birth to at a time?**
a. Four or five
b. Two
c. Eight

17. What is the lifespan of a skunk in the wild?
a. Four to six years
b. Two to four years
c. Six to eight years

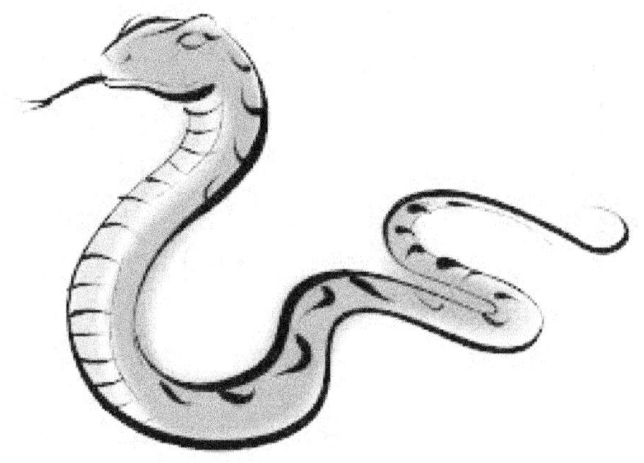

CHAPTER 46. SNAKE

1. Which is *not* a common method by which snakes kill their prey?
   a. By squeezing them to death
   b. By drowning them
   c. By shooting venom into them

2. How do snakes control their body temperature?
   a. By seeking sun or shade
   b. Automatically, by the constriction and dilation of blood vessels
   c. Automatically, by sweating or shivering

3. The bright colors of some snakes:
   a. Attract a mate
   b. Attract prey
   c. Warn attackers that they are poisonous

4. How do snakes reproduce?
    a. Most snakes lay eggs
    b. Most snakes give birth to live young
    c. All snakes lay eggs

5. Out of the 725 species of venomous snakes, how many are considered lethal to humans with a single bite?
    a. 100
    b. 250
    c. 500

6. About how long does it take for a snake to digest a meal?
    a. Several days, sometimes weeks
    b. Six to eight hours
    c. One day

7. Which snake holds the record for the largest species?
    a. King cobra
    b. Python
    c. Anaconda

8. How many teeth does a snake have?
    a. Up to 50
    b. Up to 200
    c. Up to 100

9. **How long does a snake's fang last before being replaced by a new one?**
   a. 2 weeks
   b. 20 weeks
   c. 10 weeks

10. **What does a snake use its forked tongue for?**
    a. Smelling
    b. Tasting food
    c. Capturing insects

11. **Special organs called "pits" located between their eyes and nostrils enable a snake to:**
    a. See an animal in dim light
    b. Detect an animal's scent
    c. Detect an animal's body heat

12. **How many meals does a snake eat per year?**
    a. About 30
    b. About 100
    c. About 365

13. **About how many people are killed by snakes each year?**
    a. 10,000
    b. 40,000
    c. 100,000

14. **The largest snake fossil ever found was 60 million years old and measured:**
    a. 50 feet in length
    b. 40 feet in length
    c. 25 feet in length

15. Why do you sometimes see snakes lying in the middle of the road?
   a. They're looking for food
   b. They're warming up their bodies
   c. They're hiding from predators

16. Can a snake's severed head still bite and release venom?
   a. No
   b. Yes, for up to an hour or more
   c. Yes, but only for a few seconds

17. Do snakes ever stop growing?
   a. No, they continue to grow as long as they live
   b. Yes, they stop growing once they reach a certain size
   c. Yes, they stop growing once they reach a certain age

18. What is the main threat to snakes?
   a. Disease
   b. Being taken from the wild to be sold as pets
   c. Destruction of their habitats

19. Snakes kept by people can live:
   a. Less than 10 years
   b. More than 30 years
   c. Around 20 years

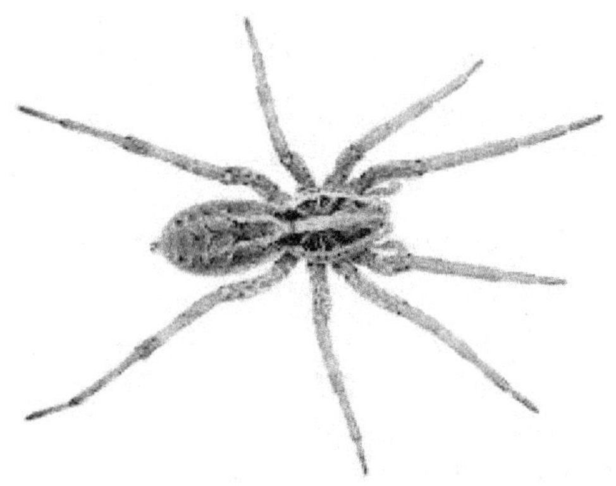

CHAPTER 47. SPIDER

1. Spiders are classified as:
   a. Insects
   b. Crustaceans
   c. Arachnids

2. How many legs does a spider have?
   a. Eight
   b. Six
   c. It varies by species

3. What is the world's largest spider?
   a. Jumping spider
   b. Wolf spider
   c. Tarantula

4. Where are a spider's eyes located?
   a. At the front of its head
   b. On top of its head
   c. On the sides of its head

5. Where do spiders have silk-spinning organs?

a. On their abdomen (back body part)
b. On their head
c. On their legs

6. Spiders' silk-making organs are called:

a. Spinnerets
b. Spigot tubes
c. Spinner ducts

7. What is a spider's dragline?

a. A thread of silk that a spider spins wherever it goes
b. A type of spider web
c. A sticky substance that spiders use to capture prey

8. How do young spiders travel to new areas?

a. They crawl away from their eggs
b. They float to other areas, carried by the wind
c. They hitch rides on other animals

9. How many species of spiders are there?

a. More than 125,000
b. Less than 15,000
c. About 38,000

10. What does a spider's front body part (the cephalothorax) contain?

a. The heart and the digestive system
b. The silk-making organs and the reproductive organs
c. The stomach and brain

11. What do most spiders feed on?
   a. Plants
   b. Insects
   c. Larva

12. What is the visual range of spiders?
   a. They are farsighted
   b. They are nearsighted
   c. They have keen vision at all distances

13. What is the color of spider blood?
   a. Dark red
   b. Greenish-yellow
   c. Pale blue

14. What do spiders use to stab their prey?
   a. Stingers
   b. Fangs
   c. Claws

15. How do spiders eat their prey?
   a. They liquefy their prey by injecting digestive
      juices into it
   b. They chew their prey
   c. They swallow their prey whole

16. Which spider is *not* poisonous to humans?
   a. Black widow
   b. Daddy longlegs
   c. Brown recluse

17. **Why did people centuries ago put spider webs
   on wounds?**
   a. To prevent infection
   b. To clean the wound
   c. To stop bleeding

18. **How long does a common house spider live?**
   a. About a year
   b. About two years
   c. About three years

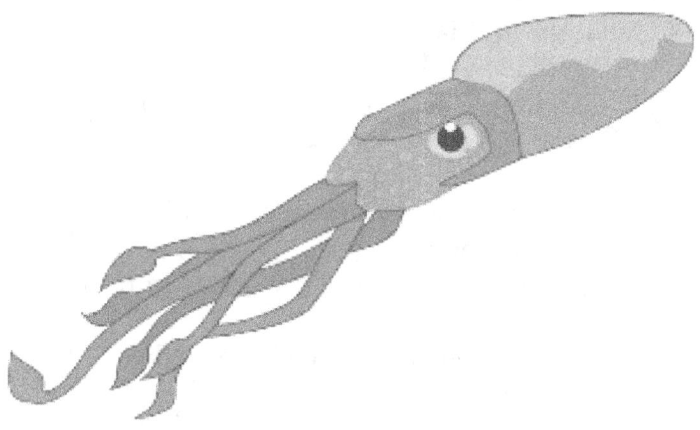

CHAPTER 48. SQUID

1. What are squid?
   a. Mollusks that live in the ocean
   b. Fish with soft bodies
   c. Aquatic mammals

2. How long can squid grow?
   a. All squid are more than 15 feet long
   b. All squid are less than 15 feet long
   c. Giant squid can be 45 feet long

3. What is the function of the suckers on a squid's arms and tentacles?
   a. To move around on the ocean floor
   b. To catch fish and shellfish to eat
   c. To sense its surroundings

4. **What do squid eat?**
   a. Plants and algae
   b. Fish and shellfish
   c. Octopuses and other squid

5. **Which is *not* a typical means by which squids avoid predators?**
   a. By using their powerful jaws to fight off them off
   b. By changing color to blend in with their surroundings
   c. By using their ink sacs to emit a dark fluid that conceals them

6. **Why is squid blood blue?**
   a. Because it lacks oxygen
   b. Because it contains a protein that turns blue when oxygenated
   c. Because it contains plasma that has a bluish tinge

7. **How does a squid propel itself through the water?**
   a. It squirts ink from its funnel to propel itself
   b. It uses its fins to swim like a fish
   c. By a system of jet propulsion

8. **In which direction does a squid move through the water?**
   a. Tail first
   b. Head first
   c. Sideways

9. How fast can some squid swim?
   a. About 12 miles per hour
   b. Only a few miles per hour
   c. Up to 25 miles per hour

**10. How deep have some squid species been
   found to live?**
   a. More than 13,000 feet
   b. More than 5,000 feet
   c. Not more than about 2,000 feet

**11. Why are some squid species able to glow in
   the dark?**
   a. Because of chemical reactions that regulate the
      balance between salt and internal water
   b. Because they have bioluminescent organs
   c. From exposure to toxins and pollutants

12. What is the squid's primary weapon?
   a. Their teeth
   b. Their beak, which is similar to a parrot's
   c. Their ink

13. Are squid social animals?
   a. Yes, they live in schools, like fish
   b. No, they are solitary creatures
   c. Some species live in schools, others are solitary

14. **What is the first step in the mating process of squid?**
   a. The female squid lays eggs (and the male squid fertilizes them later)
   b. The male squid attracts a female by means of color changes and rhythmic motions
   c. Large groups of males and females come together and start swimming in large circles

15. **How many eggs can a female squid lay at one time?**
   a. Only a few dozen
   b. Thousands
   c. Only one egg at a time

16. **How long does it take for squid eggs to hatch?**
   a. Several weeks
   b. Several months
   c. A few days

17. **What do newly hatched squid look like?**
   a. They look like miniature octopuses
   b. A small form of the adult
   c. They resemble tadpoles

18. **What is the lifespan of a squid?**
   a. Extremely short, lasting only a few weeks
   b. Quite long, with some species living for several decades
   c. Relatively short, typically ranging from a few months to a few years

CHAPTER 49. SQUIRREL

1. Squirrels eat mainly nuts and seeds, but they also eat:
   a. Mice and rats
   b. Plant matter, insects and eggs
   c. Birds, bats and flying fish

2. Why do squirrels bury extra food?
   a. They are saving it for later when food is scarce
   b. They are hiding it from other animals
   c. They will be using it to build nests

3. How much can a squirrel eat in a week?
   a. Twice their body weight
   b. Half their body weight
   c. Their own body weight

4. Where is a squirrel's cold-weather nest located?
   a. Inside a hollow tree
   b. In a tree branch
   c. Underground

5. What do squirrels *not* use their tails for when jumping or falling?
   a. For balance
   b. For attracting mates
   c. As a parachute

6. How small are the world's smallest squirrels?
   a. About seven inches long
   b. Only about four inches long
   c. About ten inches long

7. How long are the world's largest squirrels?
   a. About 36 inches
   b. About 28 inches
   c. About 20 inches

8. What gives squirrels the ability to run up and down trees very quickly?
   a. Their powerful tails
   b. Their sharp claws
   c. Their double-jointed hind legs

9. How many toes do squirrels have on their feet?
   a. Four on each foot
   b. Four on the front feet, five on the back feet
   c. Three on each foot

10. How far can squirrels jump?
   a. Up to 15 feet
   b. Up to 10 feet
   c. Up to 20 feet

**11. From how high can squirrels fall without
   hurting themselves?**
   a. About 100 feet
   b. About 75 feet
   c. About 50 feet

12. Squirrels' eyes:
   a. Can perceive only a limited range of colors
   b. Are designed to allow them to see in the dark
   c. Are positioned in a way that allows them to see
      behind them

**13. What is the fastest speed that squirrels can
   run?**
   a. About 10 miles per hour
   b. About 20 miles per hour
   c. About 15 miles per hour

**14. How many litters of young do squirrels raise
   each year?**
   a. More than four
   b. Three or four
   c. One or two

**15. How many young are generally born per litter
for squirrels?**
a. Three to five
b. One to two
c. Two to four

**16. How long do newborn squirrels live with their
mothers?**
a. Eight weeks or more
b. Two weeks
c. One year

17. Why are some squirrels considered pests?
a. They eat farm crops
b. They are aggressive towards humans
c. They make nests in chimneys

18. What is the maximum lifespan of a squirrel?
a. About 5 years
b. About 12 years
c. About 20 years

CHAPTER 50. SWAN

1. Which continent does *not* have swans?
    a. South America
    b. Australia
    c. Africa

2. Which swans have black coloration in their plumage?
    a. Southern hemisphere swans
    b. Northern hemisphere swans
    c. All swans

3. Black swans are not natively found in Europe; they were brought there in the 1800s from:
    a. South America
    b. Australia
    c. Asia

4. In what habitats are swans generally found?
   a. In the tropics
   b. In polar regions
   c. In temperate environments

5. What is the term for a male swan?
   a. Drake
   b. Gander
   c. Cob

6. What is the term for a female swan?
   a. Jenny
   b. Hen
   c. Pen

7. What is term for a young swan?
   a. Duckling
   b. Cygnet
   c. Gosling

8. What is the main diet of swans?
   a. Fish and insects
   b. Underwater plants
   c. Fruits and berries

9. When do swans typically choose mates?
   a. At two or three years old
   b. At one year old
   c. At four or five years old

10. How long do swans typically stay with their mating partners?
a. For one mating season
b. Until their partner dies
c. For two to three years

11. How many eggs does a female swan typically lay?
a. Two to three
b. Seven to eight
c. Four to six

12. How long do swan eggs take to hatch?
a. About four weeks
b. About eight weeks
c. About six weeks

13. How long do young swans typically stay with their parents?
a. Until it is time to choose a mate
b. Until they can fly
c. Until they grow their feathers

14. How fast can some swans fly?
a. Up to 60 miles per hour
b. Up to 45 miles per hour
c. Up to 30 miles per hour

15. When flying in groups, swans fly in a:
a. J-formation
b. V-formation
c. Inverted V-formation

16. What is a *wedge* of swans?
    a. A group of swans on land
    b. A group of swans on water
    c. A group of swans in flight

17. Other than humans, what are the swan's main predators?
    a. Eagles, hawks and owls
    b. Wolves, raccoons and foxes
    c. Crocodiles, alligators and snakes

18. How long can some swans live?
    a. Up to 24 years
    b. Up to 15 years
    c. Up to 10 years

CHAPTER 51. TIGER

1. Where are tigers found in the wild?
   a. Only in Asia
   b. Only in Africa
   c. Only in South America

2. What is the maximum length of a tiger, including its tail?
   a. 8 feet
   b. 10 feet
   c. 11 feet

3. What is the maximum weight of a tiger?
   a. 460 pounds
   b. 670 pounds
   c. 520 pounds

4. Based on eating habits, tigers are classified as:
    a. Herbivores (plant eaters)
    b. Omnivores (plant and meat eaters)
    c. Carnivores (meat eaters)

5. How do tigers typically hunt?
    a. In groups during the day
    b. In pairs during the day
    c. Alone at night

6. What is the primary prey of tigers?
    a. Deer and wild hogs
    b. Rodents and birds
    c. Snakes and lizards

7. How long can a tiger go without feeding?
    a. One week
    b. Two weeks
    c. Three weeks

8. How much meat can a tiger eat in one sitting?
    a. About 50 pounds
    b. About 75 pounds
    c. About 60 pounds

9. How fast can tigers run at full speed?
    a. 20 miles per hour
    b. 40 miles per hour
    c. 30 miles per hour

10. **How far can a tiger's roar be heard?**
    a. Up to a mile
    b. About one and a half miles
    c. Nearly two miles

11. **How much better is a tiger's night vision than a human's?**
    a. About six times better
    b. About four times better
    c. About two times better

12. **Which is *not* a means by which tigers mark their territories?**
    a. They scratch trees
    b. They growl or roar
    c. They use their urine

13. **Why do tigers lick their wounds?**
    a. To keep them from stinging or itching
    b. To disinfect them (with their antiseptic saliva)
    c. To remove insects and worms

14. **What is the function of the fleshy bristles on a tiger's tongue?**
    a. To help them taste their food
    b. To help them capture prey
    c. To help them clean their fur

15. **How many cubs does a female tiger typically have?**
    a. Two or three
    b. One or two
    c. Three or four

16. When do tiger cubs open their eyes?
   a. After two weeks
   b. After one week
   c. After three weeks

17. How long does a female tiger care for her cubs?
   a. About six months
   b. About four years
   c. About two years

18. How long can tigers live in captivity?
   a. Up to 26 years
   b. Up to 15 years
   c. Up to 35 years

CHAPTER 52. TURKEY

1. How long have turkeys been domesticated?
    a. 500 years
    b. 1,000 years
    c. Over 2,000 years

2. What is the primary reason turkeys are raised commercially?
    a. For their meat
    b. For their eggs
    c. For their feathers

3. What type of processed meat can be made from turkey meat?
    a. Ham
    b. Hot dogs
    c. Salami

4. What are baby turkeys called?
   a. Chicks
   b. Gobblers
   c. Poults

5. Which is *not* part of a wild turkey's diet?
   a. Small nuts and fruits
   b. Seeds and insects
   c. Grass and leaves

6. What is the colored fleshy lobe that hangs from a turkey's neck?
   a. Snood
   b. Wattle
   c. Beard

7. What is the fleshy appendage under a turkey's beak called?
   a. Snood
   b. Wattle
   c. Beard

8. What is the unique tuft of feathers on a male turkey's chest called?
   a. Wattle
   b. Beard
   c. Snood

9. What color are turkey eggs?
   a. Solid white or solid brown
   b. Blue with white spots
   c. Yellowish-tan with brown spots

10. **How long do farmers incubate turkey eggs before they hatch?**
    a. 21 days
    b. 28 days
    c. 35 days

11. **How long does it take for a male turkey to reach market weight?**
    a. About 17 weeks
    b. About 10 weeks
    c. About 25 weeks

12. **What is the average market weight of a male turkey?**
    a. 30 pounds
    b. 12 pounds
    c. 22 pounds

13. **Why can't domestic turkeys fly?**
    a. Their wings cannot support their weight
    b. Their feathers are too densely packed
    c. Their wings are too short

14. **Which is *not* a collective term for a group of domesticated turkeys?**
    a. Rafter
    b. Gaggle
    c. Pack

15. **The species of wild turkey that lives in Central America and has brilliant coloring with eyelike spots on its tail is known as the:**
   a. Eastern wild turkey
   b. Oscellated turkey
   c. Rio Grande Turkey

16. **What surprising use has been found for turkey waste?**
   a. Fuel for power plants
   b. Fertilizer
   c. Building insulation

17. **What unexpected product can contain turkey feathers?**
   a. Fly fishing lures
   b. Paintbrushes
   c. Musical instruments

18. **What is the average lifespan of a turkey?**
   a. About three years
   b. About ten years
   c. About seven years

CHAPTER 53. TURTLE

1. Where do most turtles live?
   a. In forests and deserts
   b. In ponds, lakes or rivers
   c. In the ocean

2. Approximately how many turtle species exist worldwide?
   a. More than 500
   b. Less than 250
   c. More than 350

3. What are land turtles also known as?
   a. Terrapins
   b. Tortoises
   c. Leatherbacks

4. **What is the inner layer of a turtle's shell made of?**
    a. Bony plates, which are a part of its skeleton
    b. Hardened skin
    c. Keratin

5. **What does a turtle use, instead of teeth, to cut food?**
    a. Its hard beak
    b. Its strong gums
    c. Its sharp claws

6. **Do sea turtles have flippers instead of feet?**
    a. Yes, but only in the front
    b. Yes, with the front ones longer than those in back
    c. No, they have webbed feet with individual toes

7. **How do most turtles protect themselves from predators?**
    a. Tucking their head, legs and tail inside their shell
    b. Using their powerful beaks to bite
    c. Camouflaging themselves

8. **What type of turtle primarily eats plants?**
    a. Land turtles
    b. Sea turtles
    c. Freshwater turtles

9. **Where do all turtles lay their eggs?**
    a. In freshwater
    b. In saltwater
    c. On land, in a hole the female digs

10. **What typically determines the sex of baby turtles?**
    a. The amount of sunlight the egg receives
    b. The air temperature
    c. The parents' sex chromosomes

11. **What is the lifespan of most turtles compared to other animals?**
    a. Longer than most other animals
    b. Shorter than most other animals
    c. Similar to most other animals

12. **Can turtles drown?**
    a. Only freshwater turtles can drown
    b. No, they can stay underwater indefinitely
    c. Yes, because they don't have gills

13. **Which type of turtle is considered the most dangerous?**
    a. The Florida soft-shell turtle
    b. The alligator snapping turtle
    c. The leatherback sea turtle

14. **How can turtles return to the same beaches they were born on?**
    a. They can navigate using the earth's magnetic field
    b. They rely on sight and smell for navigation
    c. They rely on the position of the sun for navigation

15. **Why do turtles seem to cry?**
    a. Tears in their eyes express sadness or pain
    b. Tears in their eyes are usually caused by eye
       irritation or infection
    c. Tears in their eyes release excess salt from their
       bodies

16. **Which is *not* a threat to many turtle species?**
    a. Hunting
    b. Pollution
    c. Lack of food

17. **What is the longest some turtle species can
    live?**
    a. 50 to 60 years
    b. More than 100 years
    c. 30 to 40 years

CHAPTER 54. WALRUS

1. Where does the walrus live?
    a. Temperate oceans
    b. The icy waters of the Arctic Circle
    c. Deep-sea trenches

2. What are walruses classified as?
    a. Marine mammal
    b. Elephant seal
    c. Amphibian

3. Approximately how long can a walrus tusk grow?
    a. About one foot
    b. About two feet
    c. About three feet

4. **What is a primary function of the walrus's tusks?**
    a. Climbing onto ice
    b. Catching prey
    c. Navigating through water

5. **Approximately how much can a walrus weigh?**
    a. More than 600 pounds
    b. More than 2,600 pounds
    c. More than 1,200 pounds

6. **What color are baby walruses?**
    a. Pale orange
    b. Grayish-brown
    c. White with brown spots

7. **What color are adult walruses?**
    a. Rusty-brown
    b. Tan with patches of black
    c. Light gray

8. **How long can walruses stay underwater?**
    a. Up to three minutes
    b. Up to five minutes
    c. Up to ten minutes

9. **How deep do walruses typically dive for food?**
    a. They feed only near the surface
    b. Up to about 1,000 feet
    c. Up to about 260 feet

10. What is the walrus's primary diet?
   a. Mollusks
   b. Fish
   c. Crustaceans

11. How does a walrus suck clams out of their shells?
   a. It uses its tusks to pry them open
   b. It uses its tongue to form a vacuum
   c. It crushes them with its teeth

12. What percent of their body weight do adult walruses eat per day?
   a. One to two percent
   b. Three to six percent
   c. Ten percent

13. Are walruses social creatures?
   a. Yes; they are highly social and form large groups called "herds"
   b. Somewhat; they tend to live in pairs
   c. No; they are solitary creatures and prefer to live alone

14. How long is the walrus's gestation period?
   a. 9 months
   b. 12 months
   c. 15 to16 months

15. **How long does a female walrus typically care for her young?**
    a. Two years
    b. One year
    c. Six months

16. **Which is *not* one of the walrus's two natural predators?**
    a. Polar bear
    b. Killer whale (orca)
    c. Shark

17. **Which part of the walrus do Native Americans of Alaska and northern Canada traditionally use to make boats?**
    a. The tusks
    b. The hide
    c. The blubber

18. **What is the literal translation of the walrus's scientific name, *Odobenus rosmarus*?**
    a. Arctic ivory hound
    b. Ocean dweller with fangs
    c. Tooth-walking seahorse

19. **What is the average lifespan of a walrus?**
    a. 10 to 20 years
    b. 20 to 30 years
    c. 30 to 40 years

CHAPTER 55. WHALE

1. Whales are classified as:
    a. Fish
    b. Mammals
    c. Amphibians

2. Where do most whales live?
    a. Oceans and seas
    b. Rivers and lakes
    c. Coral reefs

3. What is the largest animal that has ever lived?
    a. The humpback whale
    b. The bowhead whale
    c. The blue whale

4. What type of whale has sharp teeth for eating?
    a. Toothed whale
    b. Baleen whale
    c. Sperm whale

5. **What type of whale has whalebone for filtering plankton?**
   a. Baleen whale
   b. Toothed whale
   c. Sperm whale

6. **How does a whale push its tail to move itself through the water?**
   a. In a circular motion
   b. Side to side
   c. Up and down

7. **A whale's blowhole is an opening at the top of the head that:**
   a. Allows air to enter and leave the whale's lungs
   b. Allows the whale to drink water
   c. Allows the whale to hold its breath for extended periods (by closing the blowhole)

8. **How many blowholes do whales have?**
   a. Toothed whales have one; filter-feeders have two
   b. All whales have one
   c. All whales have two

9. **By what means do some whales locate objects they cannot see?**
   a. Smell
   b. Sounds (emitting them and analyzing the echoes)
   c. Touch

10. **How do whales communicate with each other?**
    a. Scent marking
    b. Body language
    c. Sounds (songs, clicks and whistles)

11. **Whales stay warm in cold water because:**
    a. They are cold-blooded
    b. They have blubber beneath the skin
    c. They have scales

12. **How is a newborn whale typically born?**
    a. Breach birth
    b. Head first
    c. Tail first

13. **How long does a female whale typically nurse her calf?**
    a. Several weeks
    b. Several months
    c. Several years

14. **Around how long does it take a whale calf to reach maturity?**
    a. 7 to 10 years
    b. 1 to 3 years
    c. 15 to 20 years

15. **What are whales' social groups called?**
    a. Gambles
    b. Colonies
    c. Pods

16. What is *not* a reason for a whale to beach
    (become stranded out of the water)?
    a. Environmental factors
    b. Injury or disease
    c. Play, courtship or mating

17. Why have whales been hunted in the past?
    a. For their blubber
    b. For meat, bones and for medicinal purposes
    c. For sport

18. How long can some whales live?
    a. 20 to 30 years
    b. 100 years or more
    c. 50 to 60 years

CHAPTER 56. WOLF

1. Where are wolves most commonly found?
   a. Northern forests
   b. Deserts
   c. Tropical forests

2. What is the average weight of an adult male wolf?
   a. 120 to 160 pounds
   b. 75 to 120 pounds
   c. 40 to 60 pounds

3. What is the typical length of an adult male wolf, including its tail?
   a. Three to four feet
   b. Seven to eight feet
   c. Five to six and a half feet

4. How do wolves mark their territory?
   a. They leave urine or they howl
   b. They leave unique scents produced by scent glands
   c. They rub their bodies against trees and rocks

5. When do wolves typically hunt?
   a. At night or in dim light
   b. During the day
   c. At any time, regardless of the light

6. What is a wolf's preferred prey?
   a. Smaller prey, such a rabbits
   b. No preference (anything it can catch)
   c. Larger prey, such as deer

7. Including bones, fur and meat, how much can a wolf eat in a single meal?
   a. Up to 5 pounds
   b. Up to 10 pounds
   c. Up to 20 pounds

8. On average, how many wolves live in a single pack?
   a. 4 to 6
   b. 6 to 10
   c. 10 to 14

9. Who leads a wolf pack?
   a. The eldest male
   b. The largest male
   c. The strongest male and female pair

10. **How much better is a wolf's hearing than a human's?**
    a. Twenty times better
    b. Ten times better
    c. Five times better

11. **How good is a wolf's sense of smell compared to a human's?**
    a. One hundred times better
    b. Fifty times better
    c. Ten times better

12. **A wolf's howl, when in harmony with others, can be heard:**
    a. Up to one mile
    b. Up to six miles
    c. Up to three miles

13. **How far can a single wolf travel in 24 hours?**
    a. Up to 54 miles
    b. Up to 124 miles
    c. Up to 96 miles

14. **On average, how many pups does a female wolf have at a time?**
    a. Two to three
    b. Four to six
    c. Eight to ten

15. **Where do female wolves raise their pups?**
    a. In a sheltered den underground
    b. In a nest of leaves and branches
    c. In a cave or hollow log

16. **Does the entire pack help with raising the pups?**
    a. No; only the parents care for the pups
    b. No; only the mother and other females help with raising the pups
    c. Yes; all members of the pack help with raising the pups

17. **How old are wolf pups when they permanently leave the den?**
    a. Three to four weeks
    b. About two months
    c. About six months

18. **Why have farmers and ranchers killed many wolves?**
    a. For profit or for sport
    b. To protect livestock
    c. To control the wolf population

CHAPTER 57. ZEBRA

1. Zebras are found in various parts of Africa, but their preferred habitat is:
   a. Grasslands
   b. Deserts
   c. Rainforests

2. How do zebras protect themselves from biting flies?
   a. By swatting them with their tails
   b. By rolling in mud
   c. By the disorienting effect of their stripes

3. Which of the following are natural predators of zebras?
   a. Lions and leopards
   b. Bears and badgers
   c. Wolves and foxes

4. How fast can a zebra run?
   a. Up to 40 miles per hour
   b. Up to 30 miles per hour
   c. Up to 20 miles per hour

5. Why do zebras sometimes run in a zigzag pattern?
   a. To increase speed
   b. To attract a mate
   c. To confuse predators

6. What type of food do zebras eat?
   a. Meat and insects
   b. Plants, grasses, and roots
   c. Fruits and vegetables

7. Can zebras see colors?
   a. Yes, except for orange
   b. No, they are color-blind
   c. Yes, they see all colors

8. What color is the zebra's skin under its white coat?
   a. White
   b. Black
   c. Striped (same as fur)

9. How many pounds of force can a zebra kick with?
   a. 500 pounds
   b. 1,000 pounds
   c. 3,000 pounds

10. **How do zebras communicate with each other?**
    a. By scent marking
    b. By using facial expressions and sounds
    c. By gently nudging each other

11. **Zebras are able to survive by drinking water at least once every:**
    a. Five days
    b. Eight days
    c. Two days

12. **How do zebras cool down?**
    a. By panting
    b. By sweating
    c. By seeking shade

13. **At what age are female zebras able to reproduce?**
    a. Two years
    b. Four years
    c. Three years

14. **The gestation period for zebras is about:**
    a. 6 months
    b. 12 months
    c. 9 months

15. **What is the average weight of a newborn zebra?**
    a. 50 to 60 pounds
    b. 90 to 100 pounds
    c. 70 to 80 pounds

16. How long after birth can a zebra walk?
   a. 20 minutes
   b. 40 minutes
   c. 30 minutes

17. How long after birth can a zebra run?
   a. 40 minutes
   b. 50 minutes
   c. 80 minutes

18. What is the average lifespan of a zebra in the wild?
   a. 15 years
   b. 25 years
   c. 20 years

ANSWERS

Chapter 1. ANT
1-c, 2-a, 3-a, 4-b, 5-a, 6-c, 7-a, 8-c, 9-b, 10-c, 11-c, 12-b, 13-b, 14-a, 15-b, 16-a, 17-c.

Chapter 2. BAT
1-a, 2-c, 3-a, 4-b, 5-a, 6-c, 7-c, 8-a, 9-b, 10-c, 11-b, 12-c, 13-b, 14-a, 15-c, 16-b, 17-b, 18-a, 19-b.

Chapter 3. BEAR
1-a, 2-b, 3-c, 4-c, 5-a, 6-a, 7-c, 8-b, 9-c, 10-b, 11-a, 12-a, 13-a, 14-c, 15-b, 16-c, 17-a, 18-b.

Chapter 4. BEE
1-a, 2-a, 3-b, 4-a, 5-c, 6-c, 7-b, 8-c, 9-a, 10-b, 11-b, 12-a, 13-c, 14-b, 15-c, 16-a, 17-c.

Chapter 5. BUTTERFLY
1-a, 2-b, 3-a, 4-a, 5-c, 6-c, 7-b, 8-a, 9-b, 10-b, 11-a,
12-c, 13-c, 14-b, 15-c, 16-a, 17-a.

Chapter 6. CAMEL
1-a, 2- a, 3-b, 4-a, 5-c, 6-c, 7-b, 8- c, 9-b, 10- a, 11- c,
12-c, 13- b, 14-b, 15- a, 16- b, 17-a, 18- b, 19-a.

Chapter 7. CAT
1-a, 2-b, 3-a, 4-b, 5-b, 6-c, 7-a, 8-c, 9-c, 10-b, 11-b,
12-a, 13-a, 14-c, 15-c, 16-a, 17-b.

Chapter 8. CHICKEN
1-a, 2-c, 3-c, 4-a, 5-a, 6-a, 7-c, 8-c, 9-b, 10-c, 11-b,
12-a, 13-c, 14-b, 15-b, 16-b. 17-a, 18-b.

Chapter 9. CHIMPANZEE
1-c, 2-c, 3-a, 4-c, 5-c, 6-c, 7-b, 8-a, 9-a, 10-b, 11-a,
12-a, 13-b, 14-a, 15-b, 16-b, 17-a, 18-c, 19-b.

Chapter 10. CROCODILE
1-b, 2-a, 3-c, 4-c, 5-c, 6-a, 7-a, 8-c, 9-b, 10-b, 11-a,
12-c, 13-a, 14-c, 15-b, 16-a, 17-b, 18-a, 19-b.

Chapter 11. DEER
1-b, 2-b, 3-a, 4-a, 5-b, 6-a, 7-c, 8-c, 9-a, 10-a, 11-c,
12-a, 13-b, 14-c, 15-b, 16-c, 17-b.

Chapter 12. DOG
1-c, 2-b, 3-c, 4-a, 5-c, 6-b, 7-c, 8-a, 9-c, 10-a, 11-a,
12-b, 13-c, 14-b, 15-a 16-a, 17-b, 18-b.

Chapter 13. DOLPHIN
1-b, 2-c, 3-a, 4-a, 5-c, 6-c, 7-b, 8-a, 9-b, 10-b, 11-c,
12-a, 13-b, 14-c, 15-c, 16-a, 17-a, 18-b.

Chapter 14. DONKEY
1-c, 2-b, 3-a, 4-a, 5-b, 6-b, 7-a, 8-c, 9-a, 10-c, 11-a,
12-b, 13-b, 14-b, 15-c, 16-c, 17-a.

Chapter 15. DUCK
1-b, 2-b, 3-a, 4-a, 5-c, 6-b, 7-b, 8-a, 9-c, 10-b, 11-a,
12-a, 13-b, 14-c, 15-c, 16-c, 17-a.

Chapter 16. ELEPHANT
1-a, 2-a, 3-b, 4-c, 5-c, 6-b, 7-b, 8-a, 9-c, 10-b, 11-a,
12-b, 13-c, 14-b, 15-c, 16-a, 17-a.

Chapter 17. FOX
1-c, 2-c, 3-a, 4-b, 5-b, 6-c, 7-a, 8-c, 9-c, 10-a, 11-b,
12-b, 13-a, 14-b, 15-a, 16-b, 17-a.

Chapter 18. FROG
1-a, 2-c, 3-a, 4-a, 5-b, 6-c, 7-a, 8-c, 9-b, 10-b, 11-c,
12-b, 13-a, 14-b, 15-c, 16-b, 17-c, 18-a.

Chapter 19. GIRAFFE
1-c, 2-a, 3-b, 4-c, 5-a, 6-a, 7-c, 8-b, 9-a, 10-b, 11-c,
12-b, 13-a, 14-b, 15-c, 16-a, 17-b, 18-c.

Chapter 20. GOAT
1-a, 2-b, 3-c, 4-a, 5-b, 6-a, 7-b, 8-a, 9-b, 10-c, 11-b,
12-c, 13-a, 14-c, 15-a, 16-c, 17-c, 18-b.

Chapter 21. GORILLA
1-b, 2-b, 3-a, 4-c, 5-a, 6-a, 7-b, 8-b, 9-a, 10-b, 11-c,
12-c, 13-a, 14-c, 15-a, 16-a, 17-c, 18-c, 19-b.

Chapter 22. HAMSTER
1-c, 2-a, 3-a, 4-c, 5-b, 6-c, 7-b, 8-b, 9-a, 10-b, 11-a,
12-c, 13-c, 14-b, 15-a, 16-b, 17-a, 18-c.

Chapter 23. HIPPOPOTAMUS (HIPPO)
1-b, 2-a, 3-a, 4-c, 5-c, 6-b, 7-b, 8-a, 9-c, 10-a, 11-c,
12-b, 13-b, 14-a, 15-a, 16-c, 17-c, 18-b.

Chapter 24. HORSE
1-b, 2-c, 3-c, 4-a, 5-c, 6-b, 7-a, 8-b, 9-a, 10-c, 11-a,
12-a, 13-a, 14-b, 15-c, 16-b, 17-c.

Chapter 25. KANGAROO
1-b, 2-c, 3-b, 4-c, 5-a, 6-a, 7-a, 8-c, 9-a, 10-b, 11-c,
12-b, 13-a, 14-a, 15-c, 16-b, 17-b.

Chapter 26. LION
1-b, 2-a, 3-b, 4-c, 5-a, 6-c, 7-a, 8-b, 9-c, 10-c, 11-b,
12-a, 13-a, 14-b, 15-c, 16-b, 17-a, 18-c.

Chapter 27. LLAMA
1-c, 2-a, 3-c, 4-b, 5-c, 6-c, 7-b, 8-b, 9-a, 10-a, 11-b,
12-a, 13-a, 14-c, 15-a, 16-b, 17-b.

Chapter 28. MONKEY
1-a, 2-b, 3-a, 4-b, 5-a, 6-c, 7-a, 8-c, 9-c, 10-b, 11-a,
12-c, 13-b, 14-c, 15-b, 16-a, 17-c.

Chapter 29. MOUSE
1-c, 2-a, 3-c, 4-c, 5-a, 6-b, 7-b, 8-c, 9-a, 10-b, 11-c,
12-b, 13-a, 14-b, 15-c, 16-a, 17-b.

Chapter 30. OCTOPUS
1-a, 2-c, 3-a, 4-a, 5-b, 6-a, 7-c, 8-b, 9-b, 10-a, 11-c,
12-a, 13-b, 14-c, 15-b, 16-b, 17-c.

Chapter 31. OSTRICH
1-c, 2-c, 3-b, 4-a, 5-a, 6-c, 7-c, 8-c, 9-a, 10-b, 11-b,
12-a, 13-c, 14-a, 15-a, 16-b, 17-b, 18-a, 19-b.

Chapter 32. OWL
1-a, 2-a, 3-c, 4-c, 5-b, 6-c, 7-a, 8-b, 9-b, 10-a, 11-c,
12-b, 13-a, 14-c, 15-c, 16-a, 17-b.

Chapter 33. PANDA (GIANT PANDA)
1-b, 2-c, 3-b, 4-b, 5-c, 6-a, 7-b, 8-a, 9-c, 10-a, 11-c,
12-a, 13-a, 14-a, 15-b, 16-c, 17-c.

Chapter 34. PARROT
1-a, 2-a, 3-c, 4-a, 5-b, 6-c, 7-b, 8-b, 9-c, 10-c, 11-c,
12-b, 13-a, 14-b, 15-a, 16-a, 17-b.

Chapter 35. PEACOCK (PEAFOWL)
1-c, 2-c, 3-a, 4-b, 5-c, 6-c, 7-a, 8-a, 9-c, 10-a, 11-a,
12-b, 13-b, 14-a, 15-b, 16-c, 17-b, 18-c,

Chapter 36. PENGUIN
1-b, 2-b, 3-c, 4-c, 5-b, 6-a, 7-a, 8-b, 9-b, 10-a, 11-a,
12-c, 13-c, 14-b, 15-c, 16-a, 17-c.

Chapter 37. PIG
1-c, 2-b, 3-b, 4-a, 5-b, 6-b, 7-c, 8-a, 9-a, 10-a, 11-b,
12-c, 13-c, 14-a, 15-c, 16-c, 17-b, 18-a.

Chapter 38. PLATYPUS
1-c, 2-c, 3-a, 4-b, 5-a, 6-b, 7-c, 8-b, 9-b, 10-a, 11-c,
12-c, 13-c, 14-b, 15-a, 16-b, 17-b, 18-a, 19-a.

Chapter 39. RABBIT
1-b, 2-c, 3-a, 4-c, 5-b, 6-b, 7-a, 8-c, 9-a, 10-a, 11-c,
12-a, 13-a, 14-b, 15-b, 16-c, 17-b, 18-c.

Chapter 40. RACCOON
1-c, 2-c, 3-b, 4-c, 5-b, 6-c, 7-a, 8-b, 9-b, 10-a, 11-c,
12-a, 13-a, 14-a, 15-c, 16-a, 17-b, 18-a, 19-b.

Chapter 41. RHINOCEROS (RHINO)
1-b, 2-b, 3-c, 4-a, 5-a, 6-b, 7-a, 8-c, 9-b, 10-c, 11-a,
12-b, 13-a, 14-c, 15-c, 16-b, 17-c, 18-a.

Chapter 42. SEAL
1-c, 2-a, 3-a, 4-b, 5-a, 6-b, 7-b, 8-a, 9-c, 10-b, 11-a,
12-c, 13-a, 14-c, 15-b, 16-c, 17-c.

Chapter 43. SHARK
1-a, 2-b, 3-b, 4-c, 5-c, 6-a, 7-b, 8-a, 9-b, 10-b, 11-c,
12-c, 13-a, 14-b, 15-c, 16-c, 17-a, 18-a.

Chapter 44. SHEEP
1-b, 2-c, 3-b, 4-c, 5-c, 6-a, 7-a, 8-c, 9-a, 10-c, 11-a,
12-b, 13-b, 14-a, 15-b, 16-b, 17-a.

Chapter 45. SKUNK
1-c, 2-a, 3-a, 4-b, 5-c, 6-c, 7-a, 8-b, 9-a, 10-c, 11-a,
12-b, 13-c, 14-b, 15-c, 16-a, 17-b.

Chapter 46. SNAKE
1-b, 2-a, 3-c, 4-a, 5-b, 6-a, 7-c, 8-b, 9-c, 10-a, 11-c,
12-a, 13-b, 14-a, 15-b, 16-b, 17-a, 18-c, 19-b.

Chapter 47. SPIDER
1-c, 2-a, 3-c, 4-b, 5-a, 6-a, 7-a, 8-b, 9-c, 10-c, 11-b,
12-b, 13-c, 14-b, 15-a, 16-b, 17-c, 18-a.

Chapter 48. SQUID
1-a, 2-c, 3-b, 4-b, 5-a, 6-b, 7-c, 8-a, 9-c, 10-a, 11-b,
12-b, 13-c, 14-c, 15-b, 16-a, 17-b, 18-c.

Chapter 49. SQUIRREL
1-b, 2-a, 3-c, 4-a, 5-b, 6-b, 7-a, 8-c, 9-b, 10-c, 11-a,
12-c, 13-b, 14-c, 15-c, 16-a, 17-a, 18-b.

Chapter 50. SWAN
1-c, 2-a, 3-b, 4-c, 5-a, 6-c, 7-b, 8-b, 9-a, 10-b, 11-c,
12-c, 13-a, 14-a, 15-b, 16-c, 17-b, 18-a.

Chapter 51. TIGER
1-a, 2-c, 3-b, 4-c, 5-c, 6-a, 7-b, 8-b, 9-b, 10-c, 11-a,
12-b, 13-b, 14-c, 15-a, 16-a, 17-c, 18-a.

Chapter 52. TURKEY
1-c, 2-a, 3-b, 4-c, 5-c, 6-b, 7-a, 8-b, 9-c, 10-b, 11-a,
12-c, 13-a, 14-c, 15-b, 16-a, 17-a, 18-b.

Chapter 53. TURTLE
1-b, 2-c, 3-b, 4-a, 5-a, 6-b, 7-a, 8-a, 9-c, 10-b, 11-a,
12-c, 13-b, 14-a, 15-c, 16-c, 17-b.

Chapter 54. WALRUS
1-b, 2-a, 3-c, 4-a, 5-b, 6-b, 7-a, 8-c, 9-c, 10-a, 11-b,
12-b, 13-a, 14-c, 15-a, 16-c, 17-b, 18-c, 19-c.

Chapter 55. WHALE
1-b, 2-a, 3-c, 4-a, 5-a, 6-c, 7-a, 8-a, 9-b, 10-c, 11-b,
12-c, 13-b, 14-a, 15-c, 16-c, 17-b, 18-b.

Chapter 56. WOLF
1-a, 2-c, 3-c, 4-a, 5-a, 6-c, 7-c, 8-b, 9-c, 10-a, 11-a,
12-b, 13-b, 14-b, 15-a, 16-c, 17-b, 18-b.

Chapter 57. ZEBRA
1-a, 2-c, 3-a, 4-a, 5-c, 6-b, 7-a, 8-b, 9-c, 10-b, 11-a,
12-b, 13-c, 14-b, 15-c, 16-a, 17-a, 18-c.